# The Face of Modern Tyranny

# The Face of Modern Tyranny

Thomas M. Carter

Illustrations by Susan Carter

**ISBN:** 9798788080277

Dedicated to my children
and
grandchildren

and special thanks to my Sister,
Susan Carter
For her invaluable support, suggestions, and
Inspiring collaboration

Other books written by Thomas M. Carter include *Badger, What He Died For: In Memory of SEAL  Mark T. Carter, SOC, USN* (Dorrance Publishing Co., 2017); and *What Is Real? My Search for Truth in a World of Chaos and Confusion* (Amazon Kindle Direct Publishing, 2019).

## Table of Contents

x

# Introduction

**I Love My Country!**

I love my country, the United States of America, and feel compelled to honor her and the traditional American values that have made her great. That is why I have written this book.

I was born the fourth of eleven children to Mark and Beth Carter at Bridger Canyon, Bozeman, Montana in 1949. My dad, Mark, was a cattle rancher, a good, hardworking, honest man. My dear mother, Beth, was a beautiful woman who bore eleven children. She literally sacrificed the better part of her life for her family. Her children were her world.  Now, there are over fifty grandchildren and over a hundred great-grandchildren.

We were not affluent growing up. We always had food, shelter, and clothing, but very few frills. I remember when Dad brought home our first TV, with "rabbit-ears" for an antenna. The picture was snowy and low quality. Our telephone was on a party line, so you could hear what another party was talking about, and you had to wait until their call ended so you could make your call.

We thrived  in the wilderness of the Rocky Mountains of Montana, picked wild raspberries and chokecherries, gathered wild mint, and fished the mountain streams for rainbow trout. We played Indians and made bows and arrows and tepees, collected Indian arrowheads from old Indian campgrounds. We gathered wildflowers that grew all over the hillsides in spring and summer. It was a magical life, but not an easy one. We had few modern conveniences. Our home was heated by a coal furnace and wood fireplace, and I remember hauling drinking water from a nearby spring in the dead of winter.

We grew up close to nature and were disciplined by her immutable laws: the "law of the harvest," hard work, "nothing worthwhile comes free," the beauty of new life, and the tragedy of the loss of life.

And all in the grand, glorious tradition of liberty and freedom!

In our family, I learned to respect the rights and desires of others. At my mother's knee, I learned about God, and from my earliest years, I loved the Bible stories she read out loud to us. I still remember my mother's prayers: "Heavenly Father, please bless all the good people in the world. And help us to do what is right."

I wanted to be a doctor from my earliest memory and carried this vision right through elementary school, high school, and college. I had the freedom to follow my dream! I learned that I had liberty to make the choices that determined my future. I learned that hard work, perseverance, and moral behavior in obedience to the commandments of God liberated me to achieve what I most wanted. I benefited from the blessings of freedom and liberty and experienced for myself the promise of America.

And then, my son, SEAL Mark T. Carter, SOC, USN was killed in action in Iraq in December 2007. Mark's sacrifice of his life for his country generated a powerful urge and commitment within me to honor and preserve and defend the traditional American values that he died for.

When I hear the current narrative that our country was built on selfishness, white privilege, and exploiting the downtrodden, I recoil in horror. I know that mistakes were made—such as the institution of slavery, the exploitation of native Americans, the internment of Japanese citizens during world war II, and more... Yes, evil people did bad things. But that was betrayal of our values by a few—not the abandonment of values and principles by the nation. We as a nation have always stood for the traditional American values of liberty, faith in God, and e pluribus unum (from many, one).

I love what this country stands for. The Judeo-Christian values and principles embodied in the Declaration of Independence and our Constitution are sound and have stood the test of time. The USA has helped millions with the precious blessings of liberty, has freed more people from tyranny, has brought prosperity and a higher standard of living to more people than any other nation in history. And not only in our own land. The USA is a beacon of liberty to the world.

It seems to me that today many people are losing confidence in the goodness of our country and are questioning traditional American values. This is so partly because of the confusions and distractions of our times, the avalanche of mass media propaganda and the collapse of trust in our public institutions, leaving many to feel cynical, inadequate or paralyzed by a sense of a futility in influencing public policy. And many are betraying these values and principles in the modern quest for money, leisure and the easy life—for placid security at the expense of liberty, for power, and a narcissistic compulsion to live for the satiety of their own selfish and carnal desires. Many have forgotten God.

For many years, I have tried to reconcile the weird situation that some of my friends whom I respect and admire as good, wonderful people have sharply differing beliefs and opinions than I. These are good people who are smart. Some of our differing beliefs are incompatible with each other so we both cannot be right! On a larger scale, it appears that America is divided right down the middle and polarized with divisive beliefs. Good people are on both sides. I really believe that most people want to do what is right. But that doesn't seem to be enough to bring us together! Is there hope for unity of belief and purpose in our divided world today? Sometimes it looks impossible, as it seems that we have stopped talking with each other and have given up trying to find common ground. Nobody is convincing anyone. So, we resort to power plays—the authoritarian impulse to settle the questions. And that leaves half of us disgruntled and angry. This is the face of modern tyranny. And we are each part of it.

I have been looking for a resolution of this problem.

It occurs to me that our only hope for unity lies not with a new President, or an ascendant political party—a powerful savior on a white horse—but within each of us as individuals—as we determine to find a true and solid foundation for what we believe. This could translate into a new era of common understanding.

3

Each of us has a responsibility for our beliefs. Our hope for unity of belief and purpose lies in the simple recognition by each of us of what is true in the confusing vortex of ideas, values and principles, and ideologies that confront us. That is what this book is about.

The contents of this book represent the accumulated wisdom of my life. I hold it a sacred obligation and honor to share what I have learned. I have no illusion that I know the truth about everything—I suffer from the same biases and blind spots that are common to mankind. But I am committed to find and embrace the truth to the very best of my ability, and I endeavor mightily to set aside my biases in favor of what is true. The best way that I have found to do that is to search diligently, listen carefully, and to treat others with respect and love.

I raise my voice in celebrating what our country stands for—for the values and principles that made her great and for what it will take to keep us great. I challenge each person to embrace the goodness of America and strive to use his/her influence to honor and preserve the greatness of this country—the last, best hope of freedom and liberty for mankind.

# The Face of Modern Tyranny

## Foreword

> The line separating good and evil passes not through states, nor between classes, nor between political parties either—but right through every human heart—and through all human hearts.
> —Aleksandr Solzhenitsyn, *The Gulag Archipelago 1918–1956*[1]

We are used to thinking of tyrannical states in terms of Nazi Germany, Soviet Russia, North Korea, or Communist China. These have been the terrible faces of totalitarianism, ruled by a military dictatorship with bloody, ruthless violence. Strong-arm rulers at the pinnacle of power and force violently imposed on the exploited and oppressed masses.

This haunting face of tyranny looms darkly on the sunset of our horizon. But the face of *modern* tyranny looms at the dawn of our horizon, rising as something quite different. Robert Kaplan, in *The Coming Anarchy*, states that "an ideology that challenges us may not take familiar form, like the old Nazis or Commies. It may not even engage us initially in ways that fit old threat markings."[2] However, this specter is ominous, dark, and just as destructive as ever: the tyranny of the mind and the manipulation of agency—the turn towards intimidation and authoritarianism through technological coercion of a

[1] Solzhenitsyn, Aleksandr I., *THE GULAG ARCHIIPELAGO, 1918-1956, An Experiment in Literary Investigation II-III*; Harper & Row, Publishers, 1975, p 615
[2] Robert D. Kaplan, *The Coming Anarchy;* Random House, New York, 2000, p 49

5

complex society—a face with a "compassionate" smile; a visage of "woke" sophistication; a soothing voice of "fairness" that exudes empathy for the marginalized and "for the children"—a subtle shift from the brute force of the past to a system of modern, managed manipulation. This modern tyranny again declares *"For the People!"* and then trumpets platitudes of fairness, equity, and social justice as it subtly captures the sentiments and acquiescence of ordinary people to assent to the policies of coercion. The tyranny that we face arises from *false philosophies* projected into *perverse ideologies* that embrace the *captivity of fear and coercion.*

But it's even more personal than that: are we not each vulnerable to the captivity of our own uninformed and flawed beliefs? And do we not each become one of the faces of tyranny as we fall into a morass of individual opinion and bias that is sometimes untethered to the usual cultural norms and institutions that bind us together with common values and principles? Thus, every man becomes a prophet unto himself, and then, adrift in a sea of doubt, ignorance, and cynicism, he is vulnerable to the false philosophies and perverse ideologies that appeal to his natural instincts. Released from the moorings of reason and tradition, he is left clinging to his own narrow interests and the creed of his immediate circle of family and friends. This is the petty tribalism that has destroyed great civilizations, and that threatens us today.

In the United States of America, we may feel that we will never accept a brutal tyrant forcing a totalitarian system upon us. *"Never will this happen to us! We are a democracy, eschew violence, and are thus impervious to totalitarianism. We are an enlightened people and will never accept tyranny!"* Mark R. Levin laments, "Unfortunately, too many among us take false comfort in the belief that there could never be a Marxist-based or oriented revolution in America, and what they are witnessing is just another in a cycle of liberal movements, which contribute to the evolution of American society and culture and, therefore, are worthy of approval and passive support. Collectively, these are America's 'useful idiots' on whom Marxists rely—that is, individuals and organizations that are unserious and unaroused by the ominous clouds of tyranny, and even worse, are participants in their own demise and that of the country."[3]

This complacency is almost surely misplaced. Kaplan asserts that "the collapse of communism from internal stresses says nothing about the long-term viability of Western democracy. Marxism's natural death in Eastern Europe is no guarantee that subtler tyrannies do not await us, here and abroad. History has demonstrated that there is no final triumph of reason, whether it goes by the name of Christianity, the Enlightenment, or now, democracy." Alexis de Tocqueville asserted in his classic work, *Democracy in America,* that, "despotism...is more likely to be feared in democratic ages, because it thrives on the obsession with self and one's own security which equality fosters." Kaplan concludes "that the democracy we are encouraging in many poor parts of the world is an integral part of a transformation toward new forms of authoritarianism; that democracy in the United States is at greater risk than ever before... History teaches that it is exactly at...prosperous times as these that we need to maintain a sense of the tragic, however unnecessary it may seem."[4]

So, we may not notice what is happening right before our very eyes: a sectarian, elitist shift to coercive authoritarianism as we lose our freedoms one by one. Like the proverbial frog in the hot water pot, we gradually tolerate, then accept, the insensible, gradual manipulations and coercions until we are scalded and boiled into paralytic obeisance. And then we suddenly discover that it is too late, that our freedoms are gone, and we are slaves to the new tyranny, the tyranny of perverse ideology, detached from the values and principles that have always been the mainstays of freedom and the bulwarks against tyranny.

Even now, we see escalating authoritarian mandates that threaten free agency, the right to congregate, the right to bear arms, and that incur an exponential burden of regulation on business. These are threats to our liberties. But it's not only the authoritarian drift—it's the tanking of the economy, inflation, supply-line difficulties, increasing taxation—all at the doorstep of ideological-driven   policies that put less money into peoples'

---

[3] Mark R. Levin. *Liberty and Tyranny, a Conservative Manifesto,* Threshold Editions, 2009, p 11
[4] Kaplan, p 60

pockets. "Money is freedom!" exclaims Bill O'Reilly[5]. And so, as the government takes over larger and larger sectors of the economy, and confiscates more and more of our assets, we are losing our freedoms.

Just as insidious and fundamentally dangerous is the new cartel of public education (unions, school boards whose members are often handpicked by unions, and business that sell curriculums and textbooks) that is forcing leftist identity politics and "woke" ideology into the heads of our children. This new disposition takes on "the substance and hard edges of a radically egalitarian ideology"[6] that "rests primarily on a charge that racial evil was systemically and deliberately embedded long ago, by the white patriarchy, in the heart of all American life, and that this ugliness thrives undiminished, which justifies all present attempts at eradication. We are not individual persons with souls; we are part of identity groups marked by special traits. We hate each other and must fight each other."[7]

This modern version of tyranny, the captivity of propaganda, division, hatred, and coercion that we are seeing, was presciently predicted by Alexis de Tocqueville, quoted here in Ben Shapiro's recent book, *The Authoritarian Moment:*

> Under the absolute government of one alone, despotism struck the body crudely, so as to reach the soul; and the soul, escaping from those blows, rose gloriously above it; but in democratic republics, tyranny does not proceed in this way; it leaves the body and goes straight for the soul. The master no longer says to it: You shall think as I do or you shall die; he says: You are free not to think as I do; your life, your goods, everything remains to you; but from this day on, you are a stranger among us. You shall keep your privileges in the city, but they will become useless to you; for if you crave the vote of your fellow citizens, they will not grant it to you, and if you demand only their esteem, the will still pretend to refuse it to you. You shall remain among men, but you shall lose your rights of humanity. When you approach those like you, they shall flee you as being impure; and those who believe in your innocence, even they shall abandon you, for one

---

[5] Bill O'Reilly, "No Spin News," October 13, 2021
[6] George Packer, "When the Culture War Comes for the Kids," *The Atlantic,* October 2019
[7] Peggy Noonan, "Democrats Need to Face Down the Woke," *The Wall Street Journal,* Nov 11, 2021

would flee them in their turn. Go in peace, I leave you your life, but I leave it to you worse than death.[8]

This, then, is the new tyranny of our day—a *soft tyranny* of subtle, ideological manipulation and coercion, and to be clear, it comes from both the Right and the Left. It leaves us confused, divided, polarized, detached and disconnected from each other, each fending for himself in a desperate struggle to protect and maintain his advantage and identity. "The challenge today is in many ways ... complicated, because (this) 'soft tyranny' comes from within and utilizes the nation's instrumentalities against itself"[9] as it "...becomes more oppressive, potentially leading to a hard tyranny (some form of totalitarianism)."[10]

This modern form of tyranny is well on its way, as we approach the brink of a chasm from which it may be impossible to retreat. **To combat and defeat it is the defining struggle of our time.**

Yet this is only the continuation of the human scene from the very beginning—the forces of tyranny have always been at play in one form or another, tapped from a fundamental human yearning to create a perfect world, a Utopia. *This is the central quest of humanity.* And the essential question is, *How to do it?* **And the fundamental debate is agency vs. coercion**, whether to empower the agency of man with truth and liberty (the democratic solution), or to manipulate, control, and coerce mankind to submit as pawns to those seeking power (the Statist, or tyrannical, solution). **And the fundamental issue is truth vs falsity.**

But, most importantly, it is an individual struggle for each of us. To paraphrase Solzhenitsyn: the line separating *freedom and tyranny* passes not through states, nor between classes, nor between political parties either -- but right through every human heart -- and through all human hearts. This query is an individual one for each person. The accumulated decisions of millions of individuals on this very question will decide whether liberty prevails.

---

[8] de Tocqueville, Alexis. *Democracy in America.* (quoted from Ben Shapiro, *The Authoritarian Moment,* Broadside Books, 2021, p 21).
[9] Levin, p 6-7.
[10] Ibid. p 18

The Face of Modern Tyranny

So, what will the new tyranny look like? The face of *modern tyranny* will be a montage of the faces of you and me as we acquiesce to the forces of coercive, managed manipulation, perverse ideologies, and to the captivity of our uninformed personal opinions. Will the image of my face and your face be reflected in this tragic mosaic? Will it be the face that we see in the mirror every day?

The Faces of Modern Tyranny

# Chapter 1: The Triumph of Ideology over Truth

When society goes mad, it's your job... to be honest and truthful about what's going on... Do not suspend your own judgment about right and wrong...for the sake of some system or some oppressive ideology or for convenience or for not being fired from work. Do not be a useful idiot.[11]

Today we are witnessing the *triumph of ideology over truth* in the devolution of political and social discourse at every level. The major issues and controversies of our time seem to be handled purely as a matter of *ideology*, rather than a careful scrutiny of what is right, what is real, and what is true. Ideology triumphs even when it clearly doesn't work as we see its policies imposed that obviously are misguided and fly against all common sense, and that end in catastrophic failure ("But our intentions were good!").[12] We worship our ideologies, and then substitute our precious opinions instead of a careful look at the facts, forgetting to remember and seriously consider our most basic and sound values and principles, and have cast aside God and His revelations in a foolish and mad trajectory of rationalization, denial and self-destruction. This is the sentinel tragedy of our time, and an indicator of really how far we as a culture and society have distanced ourselves from the moorings and anchors of reality.

---

[11] Konstantin Kisin, "In a Society Gone Mad, Don't be a Useful Idiot," American Thought Leaders with Jan Jekielek, *EPOCH TV*, 7 Sept, 2021.

[12] Ben Shapiro, "The Death of California," *Daily Wire,* Dec 15, 2021

The Face of Modern Tyranny

Every major institution seems captive to the popular "woke" ideology of the day—the Congress, the Executive, the Justice department, political parties, weak and corrupt ecclesiastical and religious leaders, academia in the universities, the corporate media (from the Right as well as the Left), the mega corporations, and now the ideological take-over of primary and secondary education by the far-left. Even science is being corrupted in some quarters by the ideological distribution of money driven by politics. Expediency reigns as we succumb to the popular mantra that seems the easiest route to the "fix" that promises short-term relief. This shallow and short-sighted policy down the path of least resistance in obeisance to the shallow ethos of the moment promises to lead us into an abyss of failure and despair.

Like the ancient civilizations that have preceded us, we distract ourselves from our failures with the trinkets and toys of technology, the unprecedented materialism of our age that puts in our possession anything money can buy, unprecedented access to that which promises to satisfy our most trivial, hedonistic and carnal appetites, and the power of communication and information technology to sift the facts and narratives we desperately want that enable us to believe just exactly what we want to believe. Meanwhile, we blind our eyes to see, cover our ears to hear, and, like the ostrich of Africa, we bury our heads in the sand with a stubborn refusal to discern the simple voices of truth that would save us. All of this is the clever distraction and manipulation of *ideology* that diverts our focus from reality and truth.

Add to this toxic brew our pride in our own wisdom, our ideological moral certainty, our virtue-signals of phony altruism, our self-righteousness that points the finger and demonizes our neighbor who disagrees, and we are entangled in a tragic vortex of contention and hatred that threatens to rise in a dark cloud of bloody violence that may end in the suicide of a once-great nation.

What then is to be done? How can this tragic vortex be turned aside?

For an answer to this question, I propose a return to first principles, to what is fundamental—the wellspring of human opinion and belief—that critical, defining point from where we diverge from one another.

12

# Chapter 2: Right vs. Left: the Insidious Trap of Ideology

You don't need an ideology[13]
--Jordan Peterson

**W**here is that critical, definitive point that people diverge in their political, social, and moral opinions and beliefs? At what moment are hearts and minds turned toward the political Right or Left, or to any opinion or belief for that matter? Where is the discernible point at which an individual's path is set? What is the fundamental imperative that will drive his or her opinions and beliefs?

I will argue that the narrative should not be set in terms of the *Right vs. Left,* or any *ideological* position. The *operative* question is more elemental and foundational. *We will never change hearts and minds by arguing and shouting at each other from the rooftops of ideology.* This has been the futile narrative of our generation that has led to hopeless division and polarization.

---

[13] Jordan Peterson, British GQ Interview of Jordan Peterson by Helen Lewis, Oct 30, 2018

Shouting from the Rooftops of Ideology

I hold that the **right question** we should be asking ourselves on any given issue is this: ***"What is true?"***—the truth question. This is the "moment of truth" that **defines the decision point that sets one's course towards opinion and belief, and is the critical juncture where our opinions and beliefs diverge from each other.**

Consider any social, moral, or political question, and ask yourself, "Where did my opinion and belief about this start?" Did it commence with reference to a familiar or customary belief system, or did it commence with a careful and focused examination of "What is the actual truth of the question?" Did you take the doctrine of your favored *ideology*, or did you invest the courage, time and energy to think it through yourself?

## Ideology, a Short-cut to Truth?

Usually, when confronted with a particular dilemma, we resort first to our favored ideology because that seems the easiest route. We naturally go to our learned and adopted frame of reference—to our mindset, our paradigm, to our

14

*ideology*: Republican or Democrat, conservative or progressive, left or right, etc. These are the colored glasses that we all wear and through which we see the world.

*Ideology* is defined in the Cambridge English Dictionary as "a set of beliefs or principles, especially one on which a political system, party, or organization is based." In our time, major ideologies have been communism, Marxism, fascism, socialism, and capitalism. More contemporaneously, conservative and progressive are ideologies that can be associated with different organizations or parties, such as the Democrat, Republican, or Libertarian parties in the United States. Ideologies can be represented on a spectrum of Right vs. Left. But an ideology can be any set of values and beliefs, not just political or moral ones, and held by individuals instead of parties. We each have our own ideology—our mindset, our paradigm, our worldview. For example, religion, health, politics, cultural norms and practices—all have ideological features. The trend in our culture today is to identify broadly with one or more of these groups, depending on the array of positions that fits one's natural sympathies, one's social or economic status, humanistic philosophy, world view, or simply what he or she has grown up with.

Ideologies become associated with a particular group, entity, party, or individual. The party or entity then becomes the face of the particular set of beliefs, values and principles. At this crucial point the party or entity bonds itself to its *ideological narrative,* rather than to the *validity* of the actual set of beliefs and principles themselves. Individuals label themselves as members of the entity or party, and the *party* then becomes the driver of their opinions and beliefs, rather than the truth or validity of the actual beliefs and principles. In this way, it easier to just accept the party's narrative on any given issue, rather than embark on a personal validation of the truth or falsity of the matter. *One's loyalty may then easily transfer from the truth to the ideology*, almost unconsciously, so he/she is now defending the ideology, not the truth of the question.

### The Deification of Ideology

I call this the *deification of ideology.* This is a very powerful dynamic! Now we worship the ideology as a *short-cut to the truth*. This is what is happening in America today--a catastrophic brew of wishful and flawed thinking, and a huge mistake. It leads to the uncertainty, confusion, and perplexed muddle of today's social, moral, and political conversations.

*Right vs. Left, Democrat vs. Republican, etc.* are *ideological* terms that distract from and obscure the critical question of *"what is true?"* When the issue is framed in ideological terms, the root of the issue, or the truth of it, is forfeited to an artificial construct. It becomes a short-cut that avoids the hard work of finding out what is actually true. When we uncritically follow the mantra of an ideology, when we *deify the ideology,* we compromise our commitment to the truth in favor of our devotion to the *ideology*. Then we are stuck in a deep rut, looking through rose-colored glasses unable to see what is real. Instead, we are defending an ideology. Thus, our *ideological* choices distract from the more important choice that we each have: **"What is true?"** and **"What is not true?"**

In this way, ideologies may actually become *obstacles* to a knowledge of what is true. The ideology becomes more important than the truth! Examples of this have been the disastrous, now fully discredited, ideologies of the twentieth century: Marxism, Nazism, communism, Maoism, all of which resulted in the captivity, torture and murder of millions of people. It is crucial to understand that most entities or organizations that assert a particular ideology eventually demand that their ideology is more important than anything else, including what is true. Thus, they fully embrace the philosophy of "the end justifies the means"—"that push-button philosophy, that deliberate deafness to suffering, (that) has become the monster of the war machine. (This is)...the betrayal of the human spirit: the assertion of dogma that closes the mind, and turns a nation, a civilization, into a regiment of ghosts—obedient ghosts, or tortured ghosts."[14] Ideological entities may distort and pervert the truth in a desperate effort to maintain themselves against all reality and any semblance of moral behavior. This is how Hitler, Stalin, and other tyrants justified and perpetuated their systems of absolute force and

---

[14] Jacob Bronowski, *The Ascent of Man,* The Folio Society, London, MMXII, pp 240-241.

16

unrestrained torture and murder. In the words of Alexandr Solzhenitsyn,[15] who survived Stalin's deadly gulags:

> To do evil a human being must first of all believe that what he's doing is good, or else that it's a well-considered act in conformity with natural law. Fortunately, it is in the nature of the human being to seek a *justification* for his actions...
>
> Ideology—that is what gives evildoing its long-sought justification. That is the social theory which helps to make his acts seem good instead of bad in his own and others' eyes, so that he won't hear reproaches and curses but will receive praise and honors. That was how the agents of the Inquisition fortified their wills: by invoking Christianity; the conquerors of foreign lands, by extolling the grandeur of their Motherland; the colonizers, by civilization; the Nazis, by race; and the Jacobins (early and late), by equality, brotherhood, and the happiness of future generations.
>
> Thanks to *ideology*, the twentieth century was fated to experience evildoing on a scale calculated in the millions.[16]

Stalin himself was a product of Leninist ideology, and he used that ideology to create his own murderous dictatorship.

> "His despotic power derived not just from his control over the formidable levers of Leninist dictatorship, which he built, but from the ideology, which he shaped...Stalin's regime was not merely a statist modernization, but a purported transcendence of private property and markets, of class antagonisms and existential alienation, a renewal of the social whole rent by the bourgeoisie, a quest for social justice on a global scale. In worldview and practice it was a conspiracy that perceived conspiracy everywhere and in everything, gaslighting itself...Stalin was blinkered by ideology and idées fixes."[17]

We think of Hitler arising as the sole tyrant arising from the ash-heaps of the First World War and the Versailles Treaty, almost as the sole perpetrator of the calamitous tragedy of Nazi Germany. Yet, history shows that Hitler was indeed a product of his time, a product of the nationalistic and authoritarian ideology that inundated Germany with roots in Hegel and Nietzsche.

---

[15] Alexandr Solzhenitsyn authored *The Gulag Archipelago,* one of the most important books of our time. Everyone should read this book.

[16] Alexandr I. Solzhenitsyn, *THE GULAG ARCHIPELAGO, 1918-1956, An Experiment in Literary Investigation I-II*, Harper & Row, Publishers, 1973, pp 173-174.

[17] Stephen Kotkin, *Stalin, Waiting for Hitler, 1929-1941*, Penguin Press, 2017, pp 901-903.

> Where did Hitler get his ideas? ...he had somehow absorbed, as had so many Germans, a weird mixture of the irresponsible, megalomaniacal ideas which erupted from German thinkers during the nineteenth century...They are not original with Hitler—though the means of applying them later proved to be. They emanate from that odd assortment of erudite but unbalanced philosophers, historians and teachers who captured the German mind during the century before Hitler with consequences so disastrous, as it turned out, not only for the Germans but for a large portion of mankind...Acceptance of autocracy, of blind obedience to the petty tyrants who ruled as princes, became ingrained in the German mind...For the mind and the passion of Hitler—all the aberrations that possessed his feverish brain—had roots that lay deep in German experience and thought. Nazism and the Third Reich, in fact, were but a logical continuation of German history.[18]

Thus, the *ideologies* extant in Germany prepared the way and facilitated the catastrophic era of Naziism. Germany, herself, was responsible. Carl Jung called Hitler the mouthpiece of the collective unconscious of the German people.[19]

And so it will be with us as we participate in the perverse ideologies of our day.

But this occurs also on a much smaller, more personal scale, with each of us, sometimes even in what some would call a pathological way, as we engage the multitude of issues and controversies that we face every day. As we experience life in all of its dimensions, we gather and cloak ourselves with the baggage of opinions and beliefs that form our own personal ideologies. Apart from the institutional ideologies extant, we each develop our own, precious and personal ideology that is at the center of our identity, of whom we see ourselves as being. This is our bias—our mindset, our paradigm, the powerful narrative within that we strive to protect, so that we may feel good about our opinions and beliefs and who we are. It affects our attitudes towards our personal relationships, health care, dietary preferences, religious beliefs, etc., many of which seem trivial or inconsequential, but *form a habitual pattern of how we shape our opinions and beliefs.* If we aren't careful, we strive to "create our own reality" in tragic captivity to our own private ideology. This is *"the*

---

[18] William L. Shirer, *The Rise and Fall of the Third Reich,* Simon and Schuster, 1960, pp 90, 92, 97, 101

[19] Carl Jung, 1938 interview published by *Omniibook Magazine* in 1942

*pathology of ideological possession"*[20] to which we are each vulnerable. This *deification of ideology* turns our hearts and minds away from the truth.

To critically look at and be willing to cast aside our personal ideology with a determined focus on what is true seems to be a herculean, and perhaps unrealistic, task. But, I believe, this is the only path that leads to a hope of being able to see things as they really are.

## The treacherous Path through Ideology

The average person in America today has little idea of how to navigate through the complex, confusing political, social, and moral landscape. He or she may be easily confused and often deceived by the conventional wisdom delivered by the mass media. This isn't because he is stupid, but simply distracted, confused and demoralized by the cacophony of the voices vying for his attention. Coupled with this is a growing cynicism that our institutions and leaders have corrupted the conversation, and that we can't trust anybody.

We live in an age of information and of technology that brings massive amounts of information to our attention. And we live in a time when "moral narcissism"[21] has overtaken our thinking, deluding us into thinking that we know everything: *in America, it seems that everybody thinks they know everything*. This is an illusion, and a dangerous one. Ask any one about their political or social beliefs and you'll hear a litany of conventional, dogmatic regurgitations of what they have heard somewhere else, and that sound good, appeal to a certain emotion, feeling, or make a certain sense to them. This is because, in the cauldron of our national discourse we have largely abandoned the search for *truth* and have embraced *ideology* instead. Indeed, as we latch onto our preferred ideology, we lose our ability to rationally think about our beliefs and discuss them with others. Then we are left with contempt for those who disagree with us, and set our priority to "winning the argument" as we descend to personal attacks instead of rational discussion. This inevitably leads to division, hatred, and ultimately to a tribalism where we are divided into

---

[20] Jordan Peterson, British GQ Interview of Jordan Peterson by Helen Lewis, Oct 30, 2018

[21] Roger L. Simon, *I Know Best: How Moral Narcissism is Destroying Our Republic If It Hasn't Already;* Encounter Books, 2016

19

opposing factions, unable to rationally discuss and solve problems together, and continually locked in irrational, hostile conflict.

We are being deluged and tempted by insidious ideologies that come to us in the form of neo-Marxist, postmodern philosophy[22] that is spawning critical race theory, cancel culture, the equity charade, polarizing identity politics, and the leftist lurch towards socialism. We also suffer from the dogmatism of far-right ideologies that seek to impose power and the far-right and the far-left violent extremists that threaten the fabric of our society. Characteristically, these perverse ideologies cloak themselves in garments of "fairness", "critical social justice", "equity", or moral outrage, and often attach themselves to well-established entities, such as a political party, or a religious or social organization. This is why it is so important that we take a close look at the ideologies that we associate ourselves with, and ask of any given idea, philosophy, or policy, *"Is this true, or is it not true?"* Do we accept the doctrine without thinking it through?

If we accept this challenge, it will surely lead us to surprising conclusions and insight about the ideology we subscribe to. There is always a mixture of good and bad, truth and untruth in any ideology, and certainly we will want to subscribe to thinking that generally reflects our own concept of the good. But it is critical that we distinguish the good from the bad, the good, better, best-- the true from the false, at the very beginning, at the outset of the controversy, regardless of the particular party or ideology. *Are we children of the ideology, or of the truth?*

So, when confronted with controversies and issues of any kind, *what is the essential **action** that leads to the truth of the matter?* Ask yourself, *"What is true, here?"*, or ask, *"What is not true?"* **This action is a choice that sets one's**

---

[22] *Postmodernism* is a new intellectual philosophy that denies absolutes: "All my analyses are against the idea of universal necessities in human existence. It is meaningless to speak in the name of—Reason, Truth, or Knowledge." An atheistic, "activist strategy against the coalition of reason and power..that seeks not to find the foundation and the conditions of truth but to exercise power for the purpose of social change." The inspirational and philosophical source of postmodernism is "within the tradition of a certain Marxism, in a certain spirit of Marxism." —from Stephen R. C. Hicks, *Explaining Postmodernism*, Ockham's Razor Publishing, 2004, pp 2-3. Postmodern philosophy has largely been adopted by the far Left.

**face towards reality or deception.** It is the "moment of truth" that sets his or her face towards the light and clarity of truth, or conversely, the darkness and confusion of error, delusion, and fallacy. **The liberating, transforming power of this action cannot be underestimated.**

The moment of truth

Here's a simple example: "Am I going to be a Nazi, or a Communist; a Democrat or Republican?" Go right to the truth question: "What is true?" at the root of this ideology. And then do your research.

Here's another example: "Am I going to get a vaccine for Influenza?" Again, go to the truth question: "Is the vaccine safe and effective?" Note that the truth question is different than the question, "Do I *want* to get the vaccine?" Or, "Do I *believe* in vaccines?" Or, again, "Do I *like* the government telling me what to do?" It's easy to mix up the truth question with other issues.

Here's another example: "Organic foods are better for me than nonorganic foods." The truth question: "What is the *truth* about the matter? Is this statement evidence-based?" Again, the truth question is different than, "I *like*

21

*the concept* of organic foods." Or, "I *want to believe* that organic foods are better." (The truth of this issue is easily found by some basic research.)

Another example: "Is climate change an existential threat?" Remember that the ideological answer on either side of the question is easier than the truth question, because it may appeal to what we want to believe, and relieves us of doing the hard research.

In each of these examples, there are popular, contemporary ideologies that would seem to answer the question. Some issues are complex. Some appeal to emotion or personal bias. It's probably easier just to take the ideology. Note that the truth of these controversies may not lie with *either* popular ideology, but may consist of elements of both. A deliberate search for the truth may even surprise you with an enlightenment that *transcends* contemporary thinking. So often, we seem to be confronted by an either/or solution that restricts possibilities of truth. But we betray ourselves and the truth if we carelessly accept the ideology without going to the truth question.

I believe that a person's choice at this point to embrace what is true, or to reject what is not true, is largely dependent on his or her commitment to truth—to accept the responsibility to be informed, to his or her willingness to do the hard work of separating truth from ideology—and most fundamentally—to his or her concept and understanding of God, and his or her willingness to keep God's commandments. Because God is at the nucleus of all questions of truth.[23] Without God, the notion of absolute truth becomes a fantasy, and we are left with nothing but our own weakness. It is a choice to accept and honor the central fact of the universe with faith and obedience to the essential nature of reality. This choice will surely transcend all ideology, politics, and the philosophies and controversies of men. **It will promise the power of truth: confidence in and the certitude of reality, and the real possibility of unity among men.**

---

[23] (Yes, I know that there are atheists who are sincere seekers of truth, but I believe that the search for truth will inevitably lead to God. More on this later in chapter 4).

# Chapter 3: What Is Truth?

The Issue in Life is Truth
—Dennis Prager[24]

B ut, this generation asks, "What is Truth?"

## The Nature of Truth

Plato described truth as knowing things as they really are. And he quotes Socrates referring to truth as "what absolutely is; the reality that is; all the invariable unchanging realities"[25]; "that reality which always is, and is not driven to and fro by generation and decay;" "eternal reality, the realm unaffected by change and decay."[26] Others have stated, "Truth is the knowledge of things as they are, as they were, and as they are to become."[27] In other words, truth is reality: past, present, and future.

The Koran states, "We cast the truth against the falsehood, so that it demolishes it, and lo! It vanishes away..." (Qur'an 21:18)

---

[24] Dennis Prager, "Fireside Chat"; Episode 194, July 2021
[25] Plato, *The Republic,"* Book V, The Franklin Library, Franklin Center, Pennsylvania, 1975, p 220, 221
[26] Ibid, Book VI, p 225
[27] *Doctrine & Covenants* 93:24; The Church of Jesus Christ of Latter-Day Saints

In the Bible, truth is likened to a double-edged sword that divides light from the darkness.[28] It is the great moderator, the great separator of good and evil. It is the ultimate certainty. The brightness of truth may illuminate our consciousness as a vision of hope and light that may become our constant guiding star.

I believe that truth is an absolute. It is sovereign, supreme, and stands above and alone as the ultimate and final arbiter and fact. Truth shines pervasively, independently, and transcends error and deception. It is not created but is self-existent. Although our perception of the truth may evolve with experience, what is true does not change from one moment to the next. We do not invent truth. Our imperative is to discover truth. The truth will not conform to us—we must conform to the truth. This can be a very daunting task!

Most of us naturally see the truth as the beginning and the endpoint of our thinking and conversation. We instinctively seek the truth of things, and that is the rock of meaning. Not so with leftist ideology. The trendy postmodern philosophy of our day embraced by the Left challenges the concept of truth. This viewpoint does not accept that Truth, per se, is an absolute. One of the Left's most prominent intellectuals, Michel Foucault states, "All my analyses are against the idea of universal necessities in human existence... It is meaningless to speak in the name of—or against—Reason, Truth, or Knowledge."[29] The postmodern project asserts that "objectivity is a myth; there is no Truth, no Right Way. All interpretations are equally valid." [30]

## Experience vs. Truth

A variation of the idea that truth is relative is that every individual has his *own* truth based on his own unique experience. But *experiential* truth is different than *absolute* truth. A real and valid personal experience may be misconstrued and misinterpreted as necessarily embodying universal truth.

---

[28] *The New Testament* ,(King James version), Hebrews 4:12
[29] Hicks, Stephen R. C., *Explaining Post Modernism, Skepticism and Socialism from Rousseau to Foucault*, Ockham's Razor Publishing, 2011, p. 2
[30] Hicks, p. 20

Thus, because *I* experience the world as cruel and ugly, the world *is* cruel and ugly. Because *I* experience life as empty and void, life *is* empty and void. Or, because when I see a spider, fear arises—that is my experience, but it does not mean that spiders are intrinsically scary. These are personal interpretations, and, although experiences are real, and may illuminate truth and reality, the interpretation of a personal experience to a generalized fact is self-evidently mistaken, because human experience is so varied and often contradictory. The challenge we all face as we mature is how to separate our false beliefs from what is actually true, and we do that by *learning from our experience*. Our experience can teach us how to distinguish truth from falsity.

We live in an age when "...what you believe, or claim to believe or say you believe—not what you do or how you act or what the results of your actions may be—defines you as a person and makes you 'good'—a narcissism of 'I know best,' of 'I believe therefore I am'...(This) moral narcissism is the reason so few people change their views about anything..."[31] Thus, we may have a vain idea that our own opinion or truth should carry the same credence as that of any other, just because we choose to believe it. The statement, "We have a different set of experiences and opinions—all are valid and deserving of respect," is true only as far as experiences are real—but just because one has an opinion doesn't make it valid or true. Yes, we should always respect others' experiences and their right to hold an opinion, but to fancy that one person's "truth" is as valid as another's, even if diverse opinions are self-contradictory and mutually exclusive, contradicts simple logic. Not much has changed since 2500 years ago, when Protagoras exclaimed to Socrates, "What is true for you is true for you, and what is true for me is true for me."[32] This comes from a wrong-headed idea that truth is internally defined by each individual rather than externally established as a foundational law of the universe. *This is a false and pernicious doctrine because it prevents us from finding truth and paralyzes us in distinguishing our own bias from the truth. It effectively destroys our ability to defend the truth.*

There is always a right and a wrong answer, or a "good, better, best" to every controversy. Our experience teaches us that. In the sea of experience, we learn

---

[31] Simon, p 12

[32] Sahakian, William S. and Sahakian, Mabel Lewis, *Ideas of the Great Philosophers*, Barnes & Noble, 1968, p 28

what works and what doesn't work. And in the cauldron of all the interpretations of any experience, we learn what is the best interpretation. There *is* right and wrong. Right is truth; wrong is falsehood. But if we can't, or won't, accept that fact, we won't be able to distinguish the "good, better, best" —the truth—much less choose to believe and act on what is true. Without acceptance of truth as an absolute, we will understand nothing, and as the Bible says, we are stuck, "ever learning, and never able to come to the knowledge of the truth."[33] To deny the reality of truth sets one adrift and drowning in the oceans of nihilism, cynicism, and despair.

Drowning in an ocean of despair

Many people are indeed ambivalent about the truth. Many are afraid of a deep dive into truth. Perhaps because of what it may reveal. They may be more interested in holding onto their precious, personal mindset or ideology, which they will defend vehemently, even as if their life depended on it. Or, they may have simply disengaged from the process out of confusion, disinterest, or discouragement. So, the very concept of truth nowadays is hard to talk about

---

[33] *The Holy Bible, The New Testament, King James Version*; 2 Timothy 3:7

and seems even futile for some, as our culture is losing its confidence that truth is knowable. Current notions are relativistic, and most people believe what they want to believe. Many have no real concept of truth, or a desire to seek it out, blissfully settling for the comfort of their own uninformed and self-serving opinions.

I will say here that it is impossible to have a successful conversation about truth unless each of the participants is invested in actually finding the truth. Minds must be open and grasping, indeed desperately seeking, what is true. Otherwise we spin our wheels in defending what we want to believe. Therefore, this book is for the truth-seekers, those rare and pure souls who, above all else, strive to see things as they really are.

The essence of truth for each person emanates from that spark of divinity within his or her soul that teaches him or her to choose and obey what is real. To nurture and honor that spark is his or her great task and privilege.

## Truth and Tyranny

Totalitarianism is necessarily and irrevocably opposed to truth and is based on profound falsity. Its very existence depends upon the lie: the alteration of reality to fit a preconceived objective. So, we must be very careful as we confront issues of truth and error. To the extent that we, the individuals participate, actively or even passively, in the untruths, the power of tyranny expands.

The mendacities of past totalitarian regimes have come to light with the clarity of retrospective vision. The murderous lies of Marxism, Leninism, Stalinism, Naziism, and Maoism have come into sharp focus over time as the deceits and falsehoods of those regimes were exposed to the world and the systems of government collapsed. History attests to the corruption of the great civilizations that lead eventually to their demise, as the lies could no longer compete with reality. Such debacles litter the dustheaps of history.

The totalitarianism of the Soviet Union has been well documented by Alexsandr Solzhenitsyn and he provides a harrowing view of the disaster of communism in Russia. He carefully documented the atrocities and murders and has offered lessons he learned about totalitarianism. He contends that the central conflict totalitarian governments provoke is one of truth vs lies. And he documents the responsibility of individuals in supporting or submitting to the lies. A careful reading of history shows that in every case, totalitarianism arose and was perpetuated not only by the violence of tyrants but by the submission and eventual support of the people. Perhaps the support was passive or was uninformed and nurtured by fear, but it eventually became willful ignorance and the pathetic submission of those who chose to avert their eyes from truth and to accept the lies. He asserts that, "it is not because the truth is too difficult to see that we make mistakes... we make mistakes because the easiest and most comfortable course for us is to seek insight where it accords with our emotions—especially selfish ones."

*As we rationalize away the truth to what we want to believe, we empower the forces of tyranny.* Without a courageous refusal to accept the lies we become part of it. Solzhenitsyn continues with a remarkable verdict:

> And how we burned in the camps later, thinking: What would things have been like if every Security operative, when he went out at night to make an arrest, had been uncertain whether he would return alive and had to say good-bye to his family? Or if, during periods of mass arrests, as for example in Leningrad, when they arrested a quarter of the entire city, people had not simply sat there in their lairs, paling with terror at every bang of the downstairs door and at every step on the staircase, but had understood they had nothing left to lose and had boldly set up in the downstairs hall an ambush of half a dozen people with axes, hammers, pokers, or whatever else was at hand?... The Organs would very quickly have suffered a shortage of officers and transport and, notwithstanding all of Stalin's thirst, the cursed machine would have ground to a halt! If...if...We didn't love freedom enough. And even more – we had no awareness of the real situation.... We purely and simply deserved everything that happened afterward.[34]

In our time we are inundated with the daily news cycle of information purporting to be the truth, but in reality is filled with half-truths, propaganda,

[34] Alexandr Solzhenitsyn, *The Gulag Archipelago*

cherry-picked facts, and outright misrepresentations in a vast sophistry of "fake news" designed to confuse, rather than clarify, mislead rather than inform, to manipulate our beliefs and opinions. In addition, we are continually exposed to the "virtual reality" of computer-chip technology, which distracts from and can actually alter the perception of reality. In such a state, the committed truth-seeker will carefully analyze information for the presence of truth, what is real, and not the dogmatism of ideology. He or she will accept a *personal responsibility* to not be deceived.

As we carefully and honestly look at our own opinions and beliefs, perhaps we will discover that we are choosing to believe what we *want to believe* rather than accepting what is true. Integrity demands that we make the choice to believe the truth. For example, this can be done by fact-checking a particular news source without political bias coming into play, rather than choosing to believe what is easy, convenient, or comforting to us. Our duty in preserving our freedom and fighting the forces of tyranny must be found in our commitment to discover truth in every aspect of our lives, and to act accordingly. In this commitment we will find the strength and means to fight the tyranny that threatens us.

## Strategies for Finding Truth:

The question is how to detach our minds from (our) narcissistic identification to see the world with clarity.[35]

Search diligently, Pray always, and Be believing...[36]

### *Search for Truth*

Many of you have already found out, and others will find out in the course of their lives, that truth eludes us if we do not concentrate our attention totally on its pursuit. But even while it eludes us, the illusion of knowing it still lingers and leads to many misunderstandings. Also, truth seldom is pleasant; it is almost invariably bitter. —Aleksandr I. Solzhenitsyn

---

[35] Simon, p 20
[36] *The Doctrine & Covenants*, 90:24

29

The truth-seeker will soon learn that finding truth takes work. Plato affirms that "he that is really a lover of learning must from his earliest years strive with all his heart after all truth."[37] It starts with a burning personal desire and commitment to accept truth wherever or whatever it may be. Then one must recognize that as humans we are vulnerable to error and deception. This is the history of humanity. Even in our own day absurd and fantastic opinions and beliefs abound. As we consider our own vulnerability to fraud and deception, we may discover some absurdities in our own thinking. This leads to an important realization: *Let us be honest with ourselves—each of us is fallible.* Our fallibility lies in our human weakness and limitation to see things as they really are, our "need to believe" what we want to believe, and our pride and passion in holding on to our opinions and beliefs.[38]

We usually hold on to our beliefs passionately, but this does not make them true. Often, we succumb to a "need to believe" that overpowers any semblance of sane thinking as we are confronted with fears, superstitions, prejudices and imagined slights--fantastic and ridiculous tales that have no connection with reality. We find ourselves *believing what we want to believe.* Nearly twenty-five hundred years ago in his play *The Sons of Aleus,* Sophocles put it this way: "What people believe prevails over the truth."

The classic 1950 film *Rashomon*, directed by Akira Kurosawa, vividly portrays the profound truth that human nature tends to "believe what it wants to believe." A husband and wife are accosted by a robber in the woods. The assailant rapes the woman, and her husband ends up getting killed, all witnessed by a woodcutter. The story is later told in court by the four participants, each with his/her own version, which markedly differ from one another. Each has an interest in telling the story from his or her perspective, each one casting the most advantageous spin. The film illustrates profoundly how one's memory and intention can be skewed into not only conscious delusion and untruth but also towards unwitting and misconstrued opinion and belief.

---

[37] Plato, "The Republic," Book VI, p 225

[38] See Thomas Carter, *What Is Real? My Search for Truth in a World of Chaos and Confusion.* Amazon Kindle Books. 2019. p 37.

Thus, *everyone has a solemn responsibility and duty to carefully examine his or her beliefs and the reasons he holds them.* It takes courage and sustained effort to distinguish whether one's motives will actually lead to knowledge of truth or cloud one's understanding of what is real. He or she will soon discover that he or she *has power over what he or she believes.* This is a crucial insight, for whatever reason, *a person's belief is his own choice.* He has agency to choose his beliefs and therefore *will be accountable for said beliefs.*

As we realize that our beliefs are really our own choice, we empower ourselves to actively choose what we will believe. *We may choose to believe what is true!* We don't have to believe just what we want to believe according to our petty whims and comfort. We can believe what is true. Further, this will "invite careful soul-searching to find what price we are willing to pay or not to pay for the truth."[39]

The ability to take a critical look at one's beliefs is a daunting task: however, if approached honestly this could develop into a *habit* of choosing to believe what is true. The habit of constantly detecting the actual truth of the controversies swirling around us is an exercise that will keep us vigilant. This may seem overwhelming at times, but it starts with our commitment to accept the most fundamental truths of our lives, and often these are the most difficult to see. With a commitment to believe what is true, the wise man or woman will give up any false or corrupted motive that leads to untruth. This is the path of integrity. We must be willing to give up our pre-conceived notions, biases, prejudices, self-interest, and any particular loyalty or relationship--even our lifestyle if necessary. We must put aside emotions that may be distracting us from clearly viewing the truth. We must become intelligently informed. We must be courageous and willing to pay any price for knowledge of the truth.

> God offers to every mind its choice between truth and repose. Take which you please—you can never have both. Between these, as a pendulum, man oscillates. He in whom the love of repose predominates will accept the first creed, the first philosophy, the first political party he meets—most likely his father's. He gets rest, commodity and reputation; but he shuts the door of truth. He in whom the love of truth predominates will abstain from dogmatism, and recognize all the opposite negations between which, as walls, his being is swung. He submits to the inconvenience of suspense and imperfect

---

[39] Susan Carter, personal communication

opinion, but he is a candidate for truth, as the other is not, and respects the highest law of his being. [40] —Ralph Waldo Emerson

The benefit of believing what is true expands our knowledge of reality and gives us power to successfully navigate the challenges of life because we see things as they really are and are not led into false beliefs. Freed from false beliefs, we are able to act consistent with reality. Beliefs that are based on truth determine correct actions, and actions when consistent with reality and truth become powerfully effective in preserving and expanding our relationships, our successes, and our ability to deal with whatever circumstances in life that befall us. In short, we overcome our world—we transcend the petty circumstances of life and become master instead of slave.

## *Standards for Truth*

*Blind is just how you would describe men who have no true knowledge of reality, and no clear standard in their mind to refer to, as a painter refers to his model.[41]* —Plato

Because human nature is fallible, and we are prone to *believing just what we want to believe, we must have reliable standards to establish and verify our opinions and beliefs*. We need a lifeline, a scaffolding, an anchor, a standard. Without dependable, steadfast, and unfailing standards, we are as an edifice built on a foundation of sand, sure to collapse when the rains of confusion and deception descend, or like a ship without an anchor, prone to drift aimlessly in the oceans of doubt.

---

[40] Ralph Waldo Emerson, *The Essays of Ralph Waldo Emerson,* "Intellect," *The Illustrated Modern Library,* p 199

[41] Plato, *The Republic*

Drifting in the oceans of doubt

There are three facets to the gold standard of truth: (1) facts, (2) correct values and sound principles, and (3) revelation from God.

## 1. Facts

Truth is usually tethered to empirically verifiable *facts.* "The truth will always be consistent with the facts" seems to be a self-evident proposition.

Our generation is the beneficiary of the accumulated factual knowledge gained over the past several thousand years and made available to those who are willing to learn. We live in the age of information, with countless facts at our fingertips. But to benefit from facts, we must be carefully and continuously informed of the facts. We must be fully engaged in knowing what is going on in the world. This takes time and effort.

Coupled with the facts is freedom of expression in the free world. Facts and freedom of thought and expression are the vital, necessary bases to rational thought and discussion. With facts at our disposal, we can create a basis for disciplined, enlightened and rational discussion. "There's a great incendiary power in facts... In this age of fingertip internet searches, the ability to checkout facts gives one great power that allows him to call in, question, or verify, whole

33

narratives."[42] Facts are as tethers to reality and to truth. As John Quincy Adams famously stated, "Facts are stubborn things; and whatever may be our wishes, our inclinations, or the dictates of our passions, they cannot alter the state of facts and evidence."

One avenue through which facts lend themselves to truth is through the study of history. As one studies the history of man, cultures, and civilizations, the facts of history teach him about the unavoidable, reliable, universal and timeless principles of life. He then can apply these lessons to his own life—in history his own life is reflected and relived. Emerson wrote that in "the grandest strokes (of history) we feel most at home...We sympathize in the great moments of history, in the great discoveries, the great resistances, the great prosperities of men; because there law was enacted, the sea was searched, the land was found, or the blow was struck, *for us,* as we ourselves in that place would have done or applauded."[43]

> The world exists for the education of each man. There is no age or state of society or mode of action in history to which there is not somewhat corresponding in his life. Every thing tends in a wonderful manner to abbreviate itself and yield its own virtue to him. He should see that he can live all history in his own person...We are always coming up with the emphatic facts of history in our private experience and verifying them here...We must in ourselves see the necessary reason of every fact—see how it could and must be.
>
> When the voice of a prophet out of the deeps of antiquity merely echoes to him (the student) a sentiment of his infancy, a prayer of his youth, he then pierces to the truth through all the confusion of tradition and the caricature of institutions...The advancing man discovers how deep a property he has in literature—in all fable as well as in history. He finds that the poet was no odd fellow who described strange and impossible situations, but that universal man wrote by his pen a confession true for one and true for all. His own secret biography he finds in lines wonderfully intelligible to him, dotted down before he was born. (--Emerson from his essay on History)

This is why it is so important to study history—for the facts, circumstances, and lessons that enlighten our own world—a window of truth that teaches and inspires and makes the world intelligible to us: "Nature is an endless combination and repetition of a very few laws," wrote Emerson.

---

[42] Dinesh D'Souza; lecture at Texas A&M University, Oct 17, 2018
[43] Ralph Waldo Emerson, "History," *Essays, First Series*

It is reprehensible that the study of history in our contemporary culture has too often been relegated to sterile facts and politically correct propaganda, informed by the ideology of the moment. Indeed, the far-left ideology of our day seeks to obliterate history and replace it with the new leftist story: Critical Race Theory, cancelling historical figures and toppling monuments, in a perverse and dishonest "theory" of history. The best history is the works that have stood the test of time: the classic ancient historians, and the modern historians who adhere to verifiable facts free of ideological manipulations and distortions.

The Scientific Method, developed during The Enlightenment, has also proven to be a reliable method of ascertaining the truth about our physical world, based on the observation of facts. The explosion of scientific and technological knowledge that has resulted in stunning advancements of understanding of our world can be attributed to the usefulness and reliability of this method. Advancements in technology of physics, computer science, communication, data management, astronomy, industry, agriculture, and medicine have transformed man's ability to control his environment and produce a way of life and standard of living never before seen on the earth. So much of our understanding of the world we live in can be credited to the systematic use of the scientific method. This has become known in our day as the benefits of "science."

Yet, the scientific method has limitations. It is dependent upon our powers of observation, which are limited to the human senses of sight, hearing, and touch—within our own time and space. We simply do not have access to all of the fundamental facts that underly the physical world.

Coupled with this, "science" in our time is in danger of becoming corrupted. Ben Shapiro describes how this happened during a national health crisis:

> While laboratory scientists did unprecedented work creating solutions for an unprecedented problem, while doctors worked in dangerous conditions to preserve the lives of suffering patients, public health officials—the voices of The Science™, the politically driven perversion of actual science in the name of authoritarian leftism— proceeded to push politically radical ends, politicize actual scientific research, and

undermine public trust in science itself...And so the authoritarian Left has substituted The Science™ for science.[44]

Postmodern philosophy discards the basic tenet of science in a rejection of objective truth. "Out of this nonsense comes the absurd belief that the scientific method and even knowledge itself are tools of the white patriarchy....Information of any kind that offends the listener is labeled 'fake news.' In reality, a nation that can no longer tell the difference between truth and lies may be facing societal decline."[45]

Even medicine, the crowning jewel of the scientific method, is being subjected to heavy doses of "woke ideology." "The national racial reckoning over reparations and critical race theory is taking over the world of medicine and health care. Prestigious medical journals, top medical schools and elite medical centers are adopting the language of social justice activism and vowing to confront 'systemic racism,' dismantle 'structural violence' and disrupt 'white supremacy' in their institutional cultures."[46] This alarming trend threatens to replace meritocracy with identity politics in our health care system.

The corruption of science in our day shows why, in many cases, bare facts are not enough. We may not know all the facts. Indeed, the facts are not always knowable, or they may be incomplete. Facts usually need context to be understood accurately. "Wrong opinions and practices gradually yield to fact and argument: but facts and arguments, to produce any effect on the mind, must be brought before it. Very few facts are able to tell their own story without context to bring out their meaning."[47] Facts may be cherry-picked or presented with prejudice to color a particular agenda.

Former VP Joe Biden, while campaigning as the Democrat candidate for the presidency, stated, "We accept truth over facts,"[48] a statement that makes no

---

[44] Ben Shapiro, *The Authoritarian Moment, How the Left Weaponized America's Institutions Against Dissent,* Broadside Books, 2021, p 98

[45] Alex Berezow, PhD, "The Slow Suicide of American Science," (/profile/alex-berezow-phd) – October 2, 2020

[46] "Medicine is Getting Major Injections of Woke Ideology," Real Clear Investigations, August 11, 2021

[47] John Stuart Mill; *On Liberty;* Easton Press, 1991, pp 31-32

[48] Joe Biden, Speech at Iowa State Fair, August 8, 2019

sense at all, but illustrates how words instead of facts can be used to manipulate a partisan narrative. Equally absurd was the Trump administration's "alternative facts" statement used during a press conference on January 20, 2017, to explain a "provable falsehood". When we put our own conception of the truth ahead of facts, we are in trouble. The use of facts requires judgment, honesty, and integrity. When advocacy uses or omits selective details, facts, and context, it denies the essential basis for debate.

This has become standard practice for the new Left, that has attacked the very existence of factual information as contrary to their conception of absolutes. Facts are no longer a tool for discovering truth, but simply a tool in an arsenal to win the argument. This is the current postmodern philosophy that seeks "...not to find the foundation and the conditions of truth but to exercise power for the purpose of social change."[49] Thus, when inconvenient, facts may be cast aside in favor of whatever works for the agenda. Words and facts are used as props to advance a particular argument, rather than to elucidate truth. Indeed, this is the outcome of a philosophy that denies the existence of absolute truth. This ideology is wedded not to truth, reality, and knowledge, but to the cynical use of words to win an argument and gain power. Of course practitioners of any stripe, including the Right, often dishonestly manipulate words and facts to their advantage. But the postmodern leftist philosophy fundamentally and explicitly denies the reality of facts, and thus feels no obligation to use them to find truth.

Indeed, we live in a time when there is a general philosophical trend against the use of facts as standards for truth. In his timely article, "The Assault on Empiricism," Wilfred Reilly laments,

> From crime to climate change, the hostility of 'movements' to data is making it impossible to address real-world problems. A remarkable aspect of today's culture war debates, across a whole range of topics, is the fact that many massively popular positions bear no resemblance to measurable truth...We live in a very postmodern era when it comes to fear and nonsense more generally, with the 'signifier' (constant media-driven panic about literally everything) bearing no resemblance to the 'signified' reality of continually improving life in our technological era. In reality, virtually all metrics measuring Western and global life expectancy, IQ, governmental corruption,

---

[49] Frank Lentricchia, quoted in *Explaining Postmodernism*, authored by Stephen R. C. Hicks, Ockham's Razor Publishing, 2011; p 3

poverty, racism, women's rights, and so forth have been improving for decades—but no one seems to know it. This rather technical and academic point matters: The more our baseline assumptions are based on (forgive me) bullshit, the less capable we are of addressing real-world problems in real time.[50]

## Mr. Reilly proposes some helpful tips:

Citizens can resist this outcome in particular, and the tide of nonsense in general, by keeping a few baseline principles in mind. First, logic and data are not discipline specific: If arguments on the left or right, or within a specific field such as education, seem nonsensical to you, they probably are. Second, academic credentials are useful as signals of probable IQ, but are very often—outside a few specialized fields like medicine—no more than that. Experts are no more immune than anyone else to extreme political bias or irrationality, and it is worth remembering that there are many experts, and they disagree about everything. Finally, most factual, primary-source information is rather easy to find...simply search (online)...and see it for yourself.

"The truth will set you free, and most of it can be found in a library.

But the use of facts is even more personal. You and I tend to seize the facts that agree with our ideology and filter out those that don't. In the ocean of factual information available to each of us, and that is paraded to our attention by the mass media, we often become overwhelmed and may engage in autopilot to receive only the facts that bolster our opinions and beliefs. If you don't believe this, try to engage a controversial subject in a circle of close friends or family with differing opinions. Every person will put forth the facts that support his own opinion, and discount or challenge the other facts that counter his belief. I tried this at a family reunion with family members with a similar overall philosophy as my own, but who disagree on certain applications. I was astounded to discover that we were unable to come to a consensus not only on the relevant facts, but on the very verity of the facts, the interpretation of the facts, and the appropriate conclusions from the facts. Each used his own set of facts (and minimized or ignored other contradictory facts) to bolster his own preconceived notions (ideology). This is why facts alone are sometimes deficient in leading to the truth.

---

[50] Wilfred Reilly, "The Assault on Empiricism," *Tablet Magazine*, 8/16/2021 (https://www.tabletmag.com/sections/news/articles/assault-empiricism-wilfred-reilly) Used with permission.

So, where does this leave us?

Facts are only one facet of the gold standard for truth. "In the realm of facts, science reigns supreme, but in the realm of values it doesn't, and you have to look elsewhere."[51]

## 2. Values and Principles

Correct values and sound principles are those that have been tried and tested in the forges of common human experience over time. They are derived from divine revelation and human experience. They offer a reliable guide to what works (and to what has always worked) and a guiding star to what is true. They are universally applicable and thus transcend ideology. They are as the rocks of reality. In times of confusion and doubt, amid the push and pull of calculating policy, correct values and sound principles provide a foundation and bulwark against the storms of deception and illusion and may act as a lighthouse to guide us through the waters of turmoil and the mists of the unknown. Correct values and sound principles will offer safety from the winds of expediency that lead to the unforeseen and unintended consequences of fallible human judgment. Sound principles should always trump expediency. "Important principles may and must be inflexible," said Abraham Lincoln at his last public address, Washington, April 11, 1865.

So, in the controversies of ideology, ask yourself: What are the relevant values and principles to this question? What are the values that I believe in? Are these values and principles consistent with each other? Are their competing values and principles? Are some more important than others?

---

[51] Jordan Peterson, British GQ Interview of Jordan Peterson by Helen Lewis, Oct 30, 2018

# Examples of Values and Principles

## Values

Peace
Love, Charity
Compassion
Forgiveness
Respect for others
Virtue
Honesty
Kindness
Diligence
Integrity
Patience
Generosity
Loyalty
Liberty, freedom
Selflessness
Friendship
Self-reliance
Provident living
Compromise
Optimism
Patriotism
Justice
Modesty
Humility
Due process
Gratitude

## Principles

-Men and women are children of God, created in His image, with inherent value as individuals, endowed with moral agency to choose between right and wrong.
- Do unto others as you would have them do to you. —Luke 6:31
-Whatsoever a man sows, that shall he also reap. —Galatians 6:7
-Men and women are responsible and accountable for their own actions.
-The rule of law, equally applied to everyone
-One must experience opposites to distinguish the good
- All men are created equal,...they are endowed by their Creator with certain unalienable rights, ...among these are life, liberty, and the pursuit of happiness. To secure these rights, governments are instituted among men, deriving their just powers from the consent of the governed.[52]

---

[52] *The Declaration of Independence*

## Principles (continued)

-The Scientific Method is a reliable way to find truth about the physical world we live in.
 -The Ten Commandments
 -Freedom of Speech necessary to a free society
-The individual has a duty to respect the rights of others
-Private property and liberty are inseparable.
-Representative government
-Men should be taught and encouraged to do good, but not forced to do good.

# Contrasting Values and Principles

| **Value or principle** | **Contrasting value or principle** |
| --- | --- |
| -Individualism | -Collectivism |
| -Love your enemies | -Despise, hate and destroy your enemies |
| -Free agency to choose | -Coercion |
| -Equality of opportunity (Liberty) | -Equity of outcome (Egalitarianism) |
| -Language is a tool to elucidate truth | -Language is a tool to win an argument or to gain power |
| -Truth is an absolute | -Truth is relative and self-defined |
| -Violence is a last resort to protect life, liberty, and property | -Violence is an acceptable method of winning an argument |
| -Means to an end must always be consistent with moral values | -The end justifies the means |
| -The traditional family unit of a married father and mother is the best unit of society | -Alternative arrangements are just as good |
| -Foundations of prosperity are hard work, right to own private property, and free enterprise | -Socialism is the ideal system to achieve utopia |
| -Men are responsible and accountable for their own actions | -Your environment, or "The system," determines your actions |
| -Look out for the interests of your neighbor | -Every man for himself |
| -E pluribus unum—from many, one | -From many, various competing with each other |
| -Fairness is an object to be sought for, but life in this world is inherently unfair. | -Fairness should be imposed everywhere by a central power |

42

One of the greatest sources of correct values and principles is a good education. Martin Luther King believed that the true purpose of education is the development of character. In a liberal education of social sciences, history, literature, and science we find a font of values and principles that have served humanity in the past and elevated and refined humanity to all that is virtuous and good.

> Ring out false pride in place and blood,
> The civic slander and the spite;
> Ring in the love of truth and right,
> Ring in the common love of good.
> -- Alfred Tennyson, from "In Memoriam"

## *A Hierarchy of Values*

In the confusing measure of competing philosophies and controversies, it is useful to establish a hierarchy of values and principles. Take any major controversy of our time and identify and prioritize the pertinent and relevant values and principles. What values and principles do you believe in, and which will you defend? Write them down and make a list. Review them carefully and think them through. Prioritize them in a hierarchy that is harmonious, internally consistent, and that avoids self-contradiction. Then one can confidently judge situations of multiple or conflicting values, or of good, better, or best solutions.

Some issues involve values/principles that conflict with each other, and can only be resolved by a compromise to middle ground, such as the conflict of pure individualism with the legitimate interests of the collective. Conversely, the altruistic ethic is often violated by the purely egoistic, or individualistic, ethic. A   middle ground is necessary. Or, the apparent dominant value or principle may hide an underlying principle, or compete with another sound, right principle. A careful scrutiny will reveal the hierarchy of values and clarify the operative principle that is really at play. For example, totalitarian governments often trumpet fairness, compassion and equality but always come down on the side of coercion.

One of the most common disagreements that I have with my leftist friends is the apparent conflict between their altruistic value of compassion and

43

benefits for the less fortunate (which I characterize as handouts), contrasted with my value of individualism and self-reliance (which they characterize as "every man for himself"). Surely, the middle ground is a compassionate ethic of caring for the poor, while "helping them help themselves" by fostering agency, personal effort, accountability and upward mobility.

Another conflicting situation is the result of greed in a capitalistic culture that rewards personal effort, which, when pursued without ethical behavior and at the expense of others, results in a general corruption of the society. The only balm for this abuse that I know of is the religious or moral ethic of honesty and treating others as you would want to be treated (the Golden Rule). Alexis de Toqueville claims that religion is necessary to motivate people to be honest.

> Liberty regards religion as its companion in all its battles and its triumphs, as the cradle of its infancy and the divine source of its claims It considers religion as the safeguard of morality, and morality as the best security of law and the surest pledge of the duration of freedom.[53]

The analysis and judgment of values and principles is a complex process of knowing the facts, having experience and mature judgment, and complete honesty and integrity. With all the conflicting information around us, it is easy to rationalize one's thinking to believe what one wants, rather than believing what is true. **This is the great challenge for each of us**—and until we do this individually with a passion for and commitment to the truth, we have no hope of unity under the banner of what is right, good, and true.

### 3. Truth Will Always Be Consistent with God-Given Revelation

Revelation from God is the ultimate source of truth and the most reliable standard of truth. Even with facts, experience, reliable values and principles at our disposal, we can be lost in our search for truth of the intangibles, the unresolved moral controversies of our time, and the origins and meaning of Life. The reasoning and wisdom of men are often utterly inadequate in answering these important questions. Montaigne discovered that:

---

[53] Alexis de Tocqueville, *Democracy in America*, p 43-44

All things produced by our own reason and ability, the true as well as the false, are subject to uncertainty and debate. "For this is a very true presupposition: that men are in agreement about nothing." For the "power of man to find what he seeks, and whether that quest that he has been making for so many centuries has enriched him with any new power and any solid truth... I think he will confess to me, if he speaks in all conscience, that all the profit he has gained from so long a pursuit is to have learned to acknowledge his weakness...For true and essential reason, whose name we steal on false pretenses, dwells in the bosom of God; there is her lair and her retreat, it is from there that she issues when God is pleased to let us see some ray of her[54]

Thus, in all the controversies of life, who will ask, What does God think?" "What has God revealed?" This fundamental source of truth and right is often calamitously ignored or rejected in favor of the preferences, whims, foibles, and purported wisdom of men.

The things that come to us from heaven have alone the right and authority for persuasion, alone the stamp of truth, which also we do not see with our own eyes, or receive by our own means...The participation that we have in the knowledge of truth, whatever it may be, has not been acquired by our own powers...It is not by reasoning or by our understanding that we have received our religion; it is by external authority and command; ...Let us bring to it nothing of our own but obedience and submission.[55]

God speaks to men through the spoken and written word of prophets, recorded in holy scripture, and through direct revelation to individuals, through enlightenment of their minds by the "still, small voice" of His Spirit. Every man has this "conscience" that speaks truth to him, if he will listen, unless that still small voice is ignored, smothered, or corrupted by a ripening of faithlessness and disobedience. God also speaks to men through the tutoring of the immutable laws of Nature and the majesty and glory of the Creation.

---

[54] Michel de Montaigne, "Apology for Raymond Sebond," *Essays, Vol II;* The Franklin Library, 1979.

[55] Montaigne. Michel Eyquem de Montaigne, also known as Lord of Montaigne, was one of the most significant philosophers of the French Renaissance, known for popularizing the essay as a literary genre. His work is noted for its merging of casual anecdotes and autobiography with intellectual insight. His massive volume *Essais* contains some of the most influential essays ever written.

The revelation of God to man is a simple and common phenomenon, understandable and available even to children. It happens every day and is the single, most powerful influence in the world that leads to truth. But it requires a sincere heart, real intent, faith in God, and a listening ear. As we carefully look at how truth is discerned, in the last instance, we must conclude that the perception of truth is a personal, spiritual experience, not a temporal or a physical one. It is intangible and communicated through the mind and the heart (not necessarily through feelings—which can be misconstrued as truth). One's spiritual eyes must be opened to fully engage in the pursuit of truth. That is why the search for truth inevitably leads to God. When the still, small voice is honored and cultivated, it leads to a miraculous epiphany of light and truth that expands the intellect and exalts the vision in a certitude of knowledge of "things as they really are." It is a spiritual experience to those with eyes to see and ears to hear--one that gives one power not only to comprehend, but to change the world for good.

> My firm belief is that he reveals himself daily to every human being, but we shut our ears to the "still small voice." We shut our eyes to the pillar of fire in front of us...The divine music is incessantly going on within ourselves; but the loud senses drown the delicate music, which is unlike, and infinitely superior to, any we can perceive or hear with our senses. —Mahatma Gandhi[56]

## Five Principles of Revelation

I speak now of my own personal experience, not as a cleric, religious leader, or having particular authority. I speak from my own observation, and from what I have learned myself.

1. Desire to know. Because God has given men agency, He communicates to those with open hearts and willing minds—those who are asking and grasping for truth.

---

[56] Mahatma Gandhi, *The Way to God, Selected Writings from Mahatma Gandhi*, North Atlantic Books, Berkeley, California, 2009, pp 67-68.

2. Faith. The initial impulse to ask of, and listen to, God comes from a spark of faith, a willingness to engage, not from a certitude of knowledge.
3. Search diligently with a sincere heart and real intent wherever and whenever you can find truth.
4. Action consistent with one's desire to know. Actions such as searching what God has revealed, praying to God and asking for help and understanding, and experimenting with actions consistent with God's commandments are manifestations of faith.
5. Being willing to learn of and accept the intangibles, the inner senses and intuitions—the still small voices that teach what is true. If you require tangible evidence for everything you believe, you will never learn the most important truths of life.

## Testing for Truth

As we carefully consider our opinions and beliefs, we must test their viability against reliable standards. The illusion of knowing the truth is so pervasive, and the will to believe what we want to believe so compelling, that we must continually test our understanding of truth against a reliable standard. Deception cloaks itself in many colors and shapes and is continually at our door to trick and cheat. Therefore, we must establish a "testing method" that transcends our own weakness and fallibility.

The testing method involves careful and courageous scrutiny of the three standards of truth, each as one facet of a precious gem—each facet is necessary for a completion of the whole. This is a discrete action that completes and verifies the determination of the truth. Is each standard or facet favorable to the question? And is each standard compatible and in line with the other standards? Each of the standards for truth when considered alone comes with perversions and phony imitations. Like a precious diamond, the gem of truth is complete only when each facet is uncorrupted, harmonious and proportioned with the others.

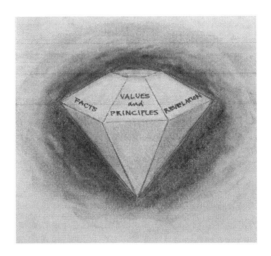

The Diamond of Truth

Another testing method is that of acting on a provisional acceptance of a perception of truth. This necessarily will involve some miscalculations and mistakes. But the fiery furnace of experience inevitably teaches and refines one's knowledge of what works and what doesn't work, what is real, and what is an illusion. Hopefully, one doesn't have to learn everything in the harsh forge of experience, but through wisdom and faith, will avoid some of the most painful lessons. Nevertheless, human experience remains a powerful and effectual domain for learning what is true.

### Revisiting your Conclusion

The truth will always sustain another look, repeated scrutiny, and under varying circumstances. The habit of revisiting a controversy is good policy. Sometimes, "the ugly dragon raises its head" only after time and repetitive scrutiny. This is why it is necessary to constantly test your perceptions of truth against the reliable facets or standards of truth: (1) facts, (2) correct values and sound principles, and (3) divine revelation. The courageous truth-seeker knows that he must continuously test and verify his or her perceptions of truth, always open to new information and insight. Only with this single-mindedness and commitment will he arrive at the confidence and certitude that will empower him to rise above the darkness of illusion, prejudice, deception and ignorance and soar into the brilliant light of truth.

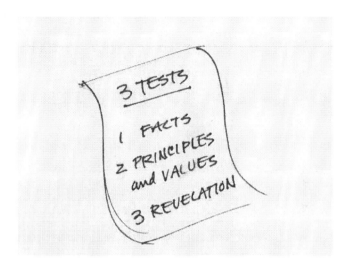

## Rejecting the Lies

The simple step of a courageous individual is not to take part in the lie. One word of truth outweighs the world.

The simplest, the most accessible key to our liberation: a *personal nonparticipation in lies!*[57]
— Aleksandr I. Solzhenitsyn

As we carefully sift through mountains of information and propaganda, we will recognize the deceptions, the outrageous, the false, and the lies. Sometimes, untruths are mixed with truths, and here is where discernment and judgment are necessary. Deception is always built with some element of truth. But when you see fibs, falsehoods, little "white lies" as scaffolding to the structure of ideology, you may clearly recognize the effort to deceive. Truth

---

[57] Alexandr Solzhenitsyn, "Live Not by Lies!"; *The Solzhenitsyn Reader, New and Essential Writings, 1947-2005,* Edited by Edward E. Ericson, Jr., and Daniel J. Mahoney; ISI Books, 2006, p558.

does not need to be supported on a structure of untruths. It will stand on its own with the foundation of honesty, clarity, full disclosure, and transparency. As we accept even the little white lies, incomplete truths, and distortions of the truth that may seem inconsequential or necessary for a narrative, we pervert our commitment to the truth. And when we excuse the lies from our own ideological masters but excoriate the lies of our adversary, we surely participate in an offense of truth.

\*\*\*\*\*\*\*\*\*\*\*

But the world today is rapidly losing its commitment to finding truth, even an acceptance that truth is knowable. Revelation from God is rebuffed out-of-hand. Traditional and time-tested values and principles are abandoned in favor of the new postmodern philosophy that favors relativism, expediency, and the politics of power. Facts are distorted or simply ignored when inconvenient. Thus, having cast off every standard and link to truth, we shout at each other from the rooftops of ideology, tossed about on the oceans of uncertainty, prejudice, self-interest, and the whims and vanities of uninspired men, blown to and fro by the storms of circumstance, tossed here and there, drowning in our ignorance of things as they really are.

# Chapter 4:  Faith and Obedience

You never know how much you really believe anything until its truth or
falsehood becomes a matter of life and death to you
--C.S. Lewis

I earlier asserted that a person's choice to embrace what is true, or what is
not true, is largely dependent on his or her commitment to truth, to his or
her personal concept and understanding of God, and his or her willingness
to obey God's commandments. It is a choice to accept the central fact of the
universe with faith and obedience.

Truly, our ability to choose what is true depends on our most inner desire to
do so. That will be coupled with a correct concept of God and the relationship
between God and man—this is the rock foundation for comprehending what is
true. This understanding may be gained by listening to His words,  His
communications with men, and the prayer of faith with real intent. Yes, there
are truth-seeking atheists that do not believe in God, but I am convinced that
the authentic search for truth inevitably leads to God. If we choose to believe
in God and are willing to learn the greater knowledge that comes from Him, we
align ourselves with the essential nature of reality and the central fact of the
universe: that God lives as our Father in Heaven, and that we are His children
with a divine destiny. As we accept this essential verity, we can move forward
in our quest for truth.

## "The truth will make you free"[58]

Today, it seems that everybody thinks they know everything. That's because the age of information and the ease of communication sets before us all that we want to hear, and we can then cherry-pick the information that supports our ideology until we feel confident that we know the truth. And we each tend to think that we have all the information that we need to answer a particular question. We all seem captive to one ideology or another that we hold passionately even as our own sense of identity. This is the *deification of ideology* and the *tyranny of uninformed opinion* that we are all vulnerable to.

But *what will it take to free a man or woman from his or her ideology?* What will it take to free you from your ideology? What does it take for men and women to fundamentally re-assess their opinions and beliefs, "to turn their backs on the rhetorical devices of emotion, invective, and hostile silence, and then to search out and speak up about the deeper reasons for holding the views they do?"[59] What does it take for someone to whole-heartedly think beyond their personal ideology in a serious search for truth? What would rock that person's world so profoundly that he or she is willing to see the world through new eyes without the blinders and bias of set beliefs?

Historically, it takes a disaster, tragedy or cataclysmic event to wake us up to what is real, to the elemental truths of life. Alexandr Solzhenitsyn suffered internment in a Siberian Gulag in Stalinist Russia: it was an experience that taught him about reality and the depths of the human soul in extreme adversity. He did not lose his faith—his experience strengthened his faith and gave him "eyes to see and ears to hear." Victor E. Frankl, author of "Man's Search for Meaning," experienced the desolation and horror of a German concentration camp. This experience forced him to see the world through new eyes:

---

[58] *The Holy Bible, The New Testament,* King James version, John 8:32
[59] William D. Gairdner, *The Great Divide, Why Liberals and Conservatives Will Never, Ever Agree;* Encounter Cooks, 2015, p 257

> Everything that was not connected with the immediate task of keeping oneself and one's closest friends alive lost its value. Everything was sacrificed to this end. A man's character became involved to the point that he was caught in a mental turmoil which threatened all the values he held and threw them into doubt.[60]

Sometimes it takes a traumatic event to shake our world so deeply that we suddenly are willing to see what is real, what is really important, and to seriously search and embrace truth; and become willing to give up our precious, personal ideology in our love for what is true. *But I hold that as men and women of agency, with ability to think and distinguish opposites, and holding the power to choose, we can act to find and embrace truth as a matter of course in our lives. Such is the challenge and the responsibility that we all face..*

But this may be an unknown path, strewn with fear, controversy, deception and doubt until step by step, line upon line, the mists of illusion dissipate in the brilliant light of truth. It will require faith as the substance of things hoped for but not yet seen.[61] This path must be an unfettered one that reverences the agency of the individual. It must be our choice to choose the truth, and in order to make a choice, we must face and distinguish polar opposites such as right and wrong, truth and untruth, good and evil. In the precarious balance of enticement to do good or evil, to distinguish right from wrong, to accept truth or untruth, *our agency empowers us to act and make the choice.* We must be free to make it real.

Thus, in our search for the truth of things, we may not always see clearly at first. Then we must reach through the fog of uncertainty, relying on the facts that we do know, the values and principles that we have confidence in, and listen to those we have learned to trust. All the while listening carefully to our inner voice, in a forward deliberate *action* of hope and faith, until the mists of illusion and delusion part, and the truth becomes clear.

This path will be marked as an intentional act of choice on the part of the truth-seeker. It will consist of serious reflection, diligent study to become

---

[60] Viktor E. Frankl, *Man's Search for Meaning;* Beacon Press, 2014, p 47
[61] *The Holy New Testament, King James version;* Hebrews 11:1

informed of facts, values, and principles, the revelations of God, and a willingness and determination to accept and embrace truth wherever it is found. It also will require, perhaps most importantly, a *willingness to change*. Hold on to what you know to be true, re-think the rest with diligence, honesty, an open mind, and a willingness to change.

Each of us will have the opportunity in the grand scheme of our lives to learn for ourselves of the transforming power of truth. Be it a life-threatening, traumatic event that wakes us up, or as a matter of course in little, mundane daily life events and decisions, each must climb the mountain of agency in choosing his path of truth vs error.

This becomes personal rather than intellectual when we experience it ourselves in the fiery furnace of life.

One must have pure motives and real intent to consistently discern truth. It has been my experience that one's ability to discern, understand, believe in, and embrace the truth is largely based upon his or her choice to embrace the truth about his or her own life, even in the intimate details that may seem insignificant, but that over time form a pattern of character. Will we be honest with ourselves? If we are not honest about the most personal and intimate aspects of our own lives, we are vulnerable to deception. Our motives will not be pure until we are willing to give up conflicted or unworthy interests, desires, passions, loyalties/relationships and dishonorable actions. For, until we do, we will be justifying or defending our own wrong behavior, instead of dispassionately seeking the truth. Neither will we be confident of our perception of truth until we have aligned our personal behavior with virtue and uprightness. Mahatma Gandhi discovered this in the crucible of his own commitment to truth.

> Man is a fallible being. He can never be sure of his steps. What he may regard as an answer to prayer may be an echo of his pride. For infallible guidance man has to have a perfectly innocent heart incapable of evil...[62]

---

[62] Mahatma Gandhi, *"The Way to God", Selected Writings from Mahatma Gandhi*, Edited by M.S. Deshpande, North Atlantic Books, 2009, p 69

54

The virtue, or righteousness, that is essential to our enlightenment of truth, springs from our willingness to be obedient to the laws of the universe, and to the laws of God. This is an act of self-surrender, of sacrifice, of complete honesty and commitment to the truth. It prepares our hearts for a great outpouring of illumination and power.

> Character is based on virtuous action, and virtuous action is grounded on truth. Truth, then, is the source and foundation of all things that are good and great.[63]

A man or woman having been stripped of his or her pride, perhaps by traumatic adversity and suffering, or by his or her choice as a child with a broken heart and contrite spirit, is in a place where he or she can listen to the incessant calls and voices of truth in the world. He or she will have new "eyes to see, and ears to hear" what they have not been willing to see or hear before. This is a profound change of heart and of perspective that will enable him/her to see the world anew. Surely, as we walk this path, our minds expand, our soul enlarges in capacity, our vision mounts, and we experience the exhilarating and transcending joy as we learn that indeed "the truth will make you free."

---

[63] Gandhi, p 26

# Chapter 5: Values and Principles of Liberty

As we commit ourselves to a path of truth, let us begin with a foundation of correct values and sound principles. Here are the foundational values that I believe will set one's face toward truth, freedom and liberty.

**Belief in God**

It all starts with a choice to believe in God and to obey His commandments. Indeed, the very foundation of the concept of right and wrong and moral standards rests with the reality of God's revelation to men and His commandments. Without God, we are left without standards or a rock to stand on. Dennis Prager reminds us that, "The death of God leads to the death of right and wrong, and ultimately to the death of universal moral standards, as opposed to feelings-based individual opinions."[64] The most thorny and tricky moral and social controversies of our time can be resolved by looking to the revelations of God.

**Love**

Love and respect for others should be the fundamental value of human discourse and relationships. "By this shall all men know that ye are my disciples, if ye have love one to another."[65] *"Always be kind"* is an appropriate motto for all of our social, moral and political discourse. When we intimidate, badger, or demonize others, we lose the ability to influence them in any positive way. Any

---

[64] Dennis Prager, *Still the Best Hope, Why the World Needs America to Triumph,* Broadside Books, 2012; p 349
[65] *The Holy Bible, The New Testament, King James version;* John 13:35

philosophy that espouses envy and hatred of others leads to bondage, both for the perpetrator and for the victim.

But love must be balanced with truth. "Do not accept anything as truth that lacks love and do not accept anything as love that lacks truth. One without the other is a destructive lie." (--St. Teresa Benedicta of the Cross)

## Free Agency

Agency is the seminal value of liberty. Without agency, the freedom to act independently is impossible. This goes to the fundamental question of humanity in its quest for a utopia: whether to coerce individuals to do the right thing, to be *acted upon* by an external force; or to empower them to *act for themselves* with agency to choose.

## Virtue

The lesson of the ages is that virtue triumphs. Virtue is inextricably tied to morality, and it is morality that enables us to live together happily. Alexis de Tocqueville asserts this fundamental core principle:

> After the general idea of virtue, I know no higher principle than that of right; or rather these two ideas are united in one. The idea of right is simply that of virtue introduced into the political world... There are no great men without virtue; and there are no great nations—it may almost be added, there would be no society—without respect for right...[66]

Indeed, the manners of most people in a nation determine the values and principles of that nation. When the manners of the people become coarse, corrupted by avarice and selfishness, degraded politics inevitably follow, and the social fabric likewise becomes corrupted. A classic historian of ancient nations, Montagu, stresses that, "Luxury is the real bane of publick (sic) virtue, and consequently of liberty, which gradually sinks in proportion as the manners of a people are softened and corrupted."[67] The rise and fall of great civilizations can be tied to the virtue and manners of the people. "Where the manners of a people are good, very few laws will be wanting; but when their manners are

---

[66] Alexis de Tocqueville; *Democracy in America, Vol I;* Alfred A.Knopf, 1945, p 244
[67] Edward Wortley Montagu, *Reflections on the Rise and Fall of the Ancient Republics,* p 100

depraved, all the laws in the world will be insufficient to restrain the excesses of the human passions. For as Horace justly observes—'Of what avail are empty laws, if we lack principle?'"[68]

I am speaking here primarily of public virtue, for private virtue can be practiced by individuals in any system of government. However, public and private virtue and morality can best be fostered under an umbrella of liberty and agency. There are many good people who are deceived by false philosophies who lead lives of integrity and goodness. The moment-to-moment and day-to-day actions of each of us display our commitment to right and virtue. But inevitably, false philosophies that disparage belief in, and accountability to, God and a moral imperative foster coarseness of manners and abandonment of worthy values (in spite of the phony virtue-signaling we often see to alleviate the guilt of unauthentic virtue). A philosophy can truly be judged by the virtue that it inspires into its followers. The discernment of real virtue requires intuition, close observation, and most of all, a personal commitment to uprightness. "By their fruits shall ye know them."[69]

## Self-reliance

A society composed of self-reliant men and women will be vibrant, creative, and energetic in preserving liberty and in doing good. Indeed, this is the seminal agency of humanity: the ability to act rather than to be acted upon. Liberty fosters the individual ability to act; tyranny creates slaves that are "acted upon" as they are manipulated to give up their own agency.

## Compassion

Empathy for each other and compassion for those less fortunate is an expression of love and respect for our neighbor. A society truly can be judged on how it cares for the poor and helpless. This value is often misplaced or perverted to justify coercion in caring for others, an abuse of agency and a hallmark of totalitarianism. True compassion not only helps those less fortunate but empowers them to use their agency to help themselves.

---

[68] Montagu, p. 46
[69] *The New Testament, King James version,* Matthew 7:20

## Honesty

"Honesty is always the best policy," quipped Abraham Lincoln. Honesty in all our communications and transactions is vital and necessary to foster trust, credibility, and the ability to work together. Indeed, honesty is a sure evidence of one's commitment to truth.

## Reason

The Enlightenment taught our world that reason can be a tool to arrive at truth. Rational discourse based on facts and correct principles is a powerful method that enables differing parties to arrive at understanding and consensus. As sincere seekers of truth counsel together, explore diverse opinions and experiences, consider opposing arguments, much wisdom and truth abound. As we look to God, using our own mind and rational powers of reasoning to the fullest, He enlightens our minds and expands our intellect to the discovery and understanding of truth in a magnificent revelatory panorama of universal truth that transcends the rational powers and wisdom of men.

## Free Speech

A fundamental value to a free society, where individuals have the right to express themselves freely subject only to limitations of safety, harm or violence to others.

**Sound principles** derive from correct values. Here are some principles consistent with and derivative from the above values:

- Men and women are children of God, created in His image, with inherent value as individuals. (A revealed truth)[70]
- Men are endowed by God with moral agency to choose between right and wrong and thus are responsible and accountable for their

---

[70] *The Holy Bible,* (King James version), Genesis 1:27

actions. (Also a revealed truth)[71] Second to the divine identity of man, this is the most fundamental and core principle of liberty, as opposite to the imperative of coercion. The primary and central question for humankind: "Will we coerce each other to do the right thing (what we want them to do), or will we teach and inspire them to do right (knowing that they will sometimes stumble)?" Will we change them from the outside in (external coercion) or from the inside out (change their hearts)?

- Men should be taught and encouraged to do good, but not forced to do good, except by laws freely promulgated by the members or elected representatives of their democratic society. This is a direct consequence of the free agency of man as being paramount versus coercion. This principle separates totalitarian systems from free governments.
- Power, dominion, or influence over others should be exercised with gentle persuasion, kindness, and patience.[72]
- "As a man sows, so shall he reap." The Law of the Harvest is an immutable principle manifested in everyday life and displayed in the resolute and unflinching laws of nature.
- "All men are created equal, ... they are endowed by their Creator with certain unalienable rights, ... among these are life, liberty, and the pursuit of happiness. ... to secure these rights, governments are instituted among men, deriving their just powers from the consent of the governed."[73] This is the fundamental principle underlying American democracy.
- From the above principle, we derive that the ideal is "equality of opportunity," distinguished from "equity of outcome," which is a violation of the principle of agency to choose and be accountable for one's choices.

---

[71] Ibid, Genesis 2:16
[72] *Doctrine and Covenants*, Section 121, v 41-42
[73] *The Declaration of Independence*

- "Reverence for Life" is a principle enunciated by Albert Schweitzer. "A principle (on which) my life has found a firm footing and a clear path to follow." –Albert Schweitzer[74]
- The Golden Rule: "Do unto others as you would have them do unto you."
- The rule of law, and that no-one is above the law, championed by Abraham Lincoln:

  Let reverence for the **laws**, be breathed by every American mother, to the lisping babe, that prattles on her lap – let it be taught in schools, in seminaries, and in colleges; let it be written in Primmers, spelling books, and in Almanacs; let it be preached from the pulpit, proclaimed in legislative halls, and enforced in courts of justice... Let every man remember that to violate the **law**, is to trample on the blood of his father, and to tear the character of his own, and his children's liberty.

- "By their fruits, ye shall know them"—the fundamental test of any individual, system, culture, or government.
- Representative government that reflects the will of the majority of the people. Works best when closest to the people, as in local government.

These tried-and-true core values and principles are fundamental to the establishment and preservation of freedom and liberty. They form the bedrock principled foundation of a free society.

Today, they are under attack as never before by those that seek to tear down the very foundations of Judeo-Christian culture and replace it with a secular and tyrannical socialistic system. We see this in the postmodern, neomarxist philosophy of the far Left that is teaching Critical Race Theory, white supremacy and espousing identity politics. But there are creeping forms of authoritarianism happening in America from both the Right and the Left, and from individuals of any stripe who are seeking to gain power and exercise control over the actions of others. These destructive ideologies can be

---

[74] Albert Schweitzer, *Out of My Life and Thought.* Easton Press 1989, p. 219

identified by a close examination of the underlying values and principles that they are built upon, which is the subject of the next chapter.

# Chapter 6:  Values and Principles of Tyranny

The modern progressive speaks the language of high-minded purpose but always ends with coercion.
—Wall Street Journal[75]

Although tyrannical systems speak platitudes of virtue, fairness, equality, "for the people", and "for the children," a close examination of their values and principles will reveal undercurrents of power and coercion that clarify the true nature of their agenda. This requires an alert and open mind that is searching for truth. Again, the essential, primary questions are: "What is true?" and "What is not true?"

Make no mistake about it, the threats to our liberty come from elements of both the Right and the Left, whenever and wherever correct values and sound principles are violated. It is not my purpose to accuse or demonize any particular party, but to identify the values and principles that must be maintained to protect our liberty, and expose those that will inevitably lead to its destruction. People have their own responsibility to identify their own particular values and principles, and then compare them to the ideology that they are embracing, or contemplating to embrace. (A word of caution: people are usually much more forgiving of the violations from their own ideological group than those of whom they disagree with. Integrity demands that one calls out violations of values and principles wherever they exist.)

---

[75] WSJ Editorial Board, "Your Vaccine Papers, Please," *Wall Street Journal*, August 3, 2021

Here is a short list of the values and principles that seem to be characteristic of tyrannical systems:

**Atheism:** Tyranny of necessity denies the existence of God. Tyrants set themselves up as a god with authority and power to compel the actions of others. (Sometimes they do this actually in the name of God, claiming to be a believer, but actually in name only, substituting their own wisdom for the commandments of God.) Totalitarian philosophy is essentially godless, denying the supremacy and authority of the creator and father of the human race, substituting a powerful, secular government.

Socialism is a form of tyranny, disguised as a benevolent, but man-made, force imposing equality, but in essence requires a powerful secular central government of coercion. Fyodor Dostoevsky in his famous novel, *The Brothers Karamazov"* states, "For  socialism is not merely the labour (sic) question, or the question of the so-called fourth estate, it is above all things the atheistic question, the question of the form taken by atheism today, the question of the tower of Babel built without God, not to mount to heaven from earth but to bring heaven down to earth."[76]

**Coercion** is the core tool of tyranny. Tyranny always involves the loss of agency, whether forcibly taken or manipulated, or given up voluntarily and foolishly out of deception or fear. This dynamic is usually obscured or hidden in the interest of a desirable outcome such as in the popular mantra: "For the People!" Hillary Clinton while running for president in 2016 famously said, "We are not trying to change peoples' hearts. We want to change the system!" The "system" for tyrants is an entity of coercion, forcing men to do what *they* believe is the right thing.

This can take place even to the extent of enforcing altruism, a most insidious form of coercion—making people do the right thing. A recent article in *The Atlantic,*  "Sometimes Altruism Needs to be Enforced,"[77] epitomizes the

---

[76] Fyodor Dostoevsky, *The Brothers Karamazov;* The Easton Press, 1979, p 18

[77] Nicholas A. Christakis, "Sometimes Altruism Needs to Be Enforced," *The Atlantic,* October 20, 2021

haughty and self-righteous attitude of the elites to make sure we are all doing the right thing:

> But what if individual motivations and gentle forces are not enough? Here, the interpersonal nature of contagious disease—namely that individual actions that increase or reduce one's personal risk at the same time increase or reduce the risks one imposes on *others*—creates the collective-action problem in the first place and justifies more forceful, even coercive, measures by schools, work sites, and the government...we may need to deploy them...One must be willing to leverage the full range of our evolutionary impulses toward cooperation. Some of these less appealing evolutionary capacities for enforcing cooperation...may be required.

Yes, laws designed for the good of society are necessary, but in a free society such laws are promulgated by freely elected representatives of the people, and, when legislated beyond reasonable bounds of liberty, can be changed by the voice of the people.

**Power:** This is the fundamental dynamic of tyrannical entities—the lust for power. Because tyrannical philosophy does not believe in truth as an absolute, and that men are agents unto themselves, the only tangible reality for them is power—to shape the world according to their own vision.

**Government by Ideology** rather than from sound values and principles: values such as liberty and equality of opportunity—and principles such as free agency and representative government. We see this today as administrations blindly elevate their ideological philosophy and commitment as more important than what is true—even when it clearly isn't working. The "Green New Deal" of the Democrat party is a good example of how an impractical ideology morphs into religious zeal at the expense of all other interests, trampling on the liberties of a free society.

**"The end justifies the means":** A characteristic of totalitarian systems that places supreme confidence in their worthy "end" and sacrifices correct values and principles to get there. We see this in our time in the unscrupulous demonization of opposing parties, justified by righteous intent (from both the Right and the Left). This is a malicious and evil doctrine that has delivered the suffering and death of untold millions as tyrants seek to justify what they know is wrong in the interest of a perceived worthy, virtuous, or lofty goal. This is the history of lies, deceptions, tortures, genocide, and ruinous tyranny—the product of ideology divorced from virtue and from morality.

**Fear and Violence:** Tyrannical coercion necessarily involves fear and violence as tools of choice--the short-cut to an end that would never be achieved through rational dialogue and free choice. Violence may be explicit or implicit, active or passive, but certainly coercive, and always reinforced with fear. We see this already in our country in the form of various violent extremist groups: from the Left: Antifa and Black Lives Matter, and from the Right: QAnon and The Proud Boys. This dynamic in passive form is also in play whenever we as individuals try to force (impose) our views (ideology) on others.

**Equity in the name of Equality**. Equality of opportunity and equal under the law are indeed  seminal values of liberty and freedom. Men must have equal opportunity to follow their dreams and freedom to live their lives according to their own choices. **Equity of outcome** is the new mantra of those who stand to gain power by forcing equal outcomes regardless of the choices inherent in a free society. It is another variation of the old authoritarian impulse to force people to be equal instead of providing equal opportunity. Inequality of outcome will always be present in a free society as the consequence of the free choices made by individuals who express their agency in one way or the other. But to suppress agency in the interest of equity is to mount the slippery slope to tyranny.

**Denial of objective reality (truth) and the futility of reason:** Postmodern philosophy does not believe in the objective reality of truth. Therefore, reason is futile. "Once we set aside reality and reason, what are we left with to go on?"[78] We are left to follow our feelings, instincts, and irrational commitments to an ideology, an ideology based on an impulse to power. Bereft of truth and

---

[78] Stephen R. C. Hicks, *Explaining Postmodernism, Skepticism and Socialism from Rousseau to Foucault;* Ockham's Razor Publishing, 2018, p 82

reason, the appeal to feelings and instincts leads to helpless confusion and chaos. The tyrant is eager to step in with an exercise of power.

**Expediency Trumping Principle:** To the authoritarian, sound principles can be discarded in the interest of expediency for a worthy end. A great example of this is when President George Bush famously declared, "I've abandoned free-market principles to save the free market system"[79] during a 2008 interview as he discussed his administration's economic interventions in the wake of the financial crisis. One could argue that President Bush abandoned principle for an expedient short-term benefit to "save the economy". It's tempting to abandon correct principles when expediency seems the easier or better way to go. That is when it is more important than ever to uphold the principle. Principles should always trump expediency.

**Identity Politics—the unequal application of the law:** The totalitarian group applies the law differently according to its favored elites. We have seen this from the Right in recent years when conservative principles were betrayed in favor of special interests. Now, the exploitation of minorities and disadvantaged groups in order to gain power is happening in the guise of repairing past injustice. This is a frank violation of the principle of equality of opportunity in favor of equity of outcome requiring that favored groups be treated differently, according to differences of race, religion, or personal characteristics. This is the identity politics game.

According to this philosophy, "individuals are not in control of their feelings: their identities are a product of their group memberships, whether economic, sexual, or racial."[80] A person's race, sex, or other group membership most deeply shapes his/her views and feelings. Individuals are unable to think and act independently separate from their group. Thus the "group" deserves special treatment. This is the basis of the "identity politics" fracas that the Left is playing, stemming from their fundamental belief that human behavior is directed by environment and socioeconomic interest, not by man as an agent unto himself.

---

[79] Candy Crowley interview with George W. Bush, "Bush on Economy, Iraq, Legacy," CNN, Dec 16, 2008

[80] Hicks, p 82

Identity groups pit one group against another. Hicks explains why:

"Since the shaping economic, sexual, or racial experiences or developments vary from group to group, differing groups have no common experiential framework. With no objective standard by which to mediate their different perspectives and feeling, and with no appeal to reason possible, group balkanization and conflict must necessarily result... Nasty political correctness as a tactic then makes perfect sense. Having rejected reason, we will not expect ourselves or others to behave reasonably. Having put our passions to the fore, we will act and react more crudely and range-of-the-moment. Having lost our sense of ourselves as individuals, we will seek our identities in our groups. Having little in common with different groups, we will see them as competitive enemies. Having abandoned recourse to rational and neutral standards, violent competition will seem practical. And having abandoned peaceful conflict resolution, prudence will dictate that only the most ruthless will survive."[81]

Identity politics leads to envy, hatred, violence and chaos as group competitions for influence, divorced from truth and reason, become brutal power plays.

**Fairness** is a term bandied about and abused so frequently that it has almost become a signal of tyrannical intent. "It isn't fair!" the children whine. And the adult replies, "Whoever promised you that life would be fair?" People of good intent will always strive for fairness, but will also recognize that the ideal of fairness is a promise  of the next world, not this one, that coerced fairness violates agency and the ethic of personal responsibility, and destroys liberty. The tyrant gains power by promising fairness but never quite makes that happen, in spite of dictatorial mandates that crush liberty and agency. Indeed, the imposition of fairness in this world inexorably crushes the human spirit, the most unfair result of all. A great example of this was the imposition of socialistic equality (fairness) by  the communist party in Soviet Russia during the Stalin era. Millions of people were murdered or carted off to the Siberian Gulag in abject slavery, while millions more perished from starvation. All in the name of fairness.

---

[81] Hicks, pp 82-83

**"For the People"** is another platitude that, when proclaimed, is almost always a cover for a tyrannical ploy in the interests of a particular group or person. Policies that promote prosperity, freedom and liberty almost always will stand by themselves, needing no such proclamation.

**Intolerance** of others' opinions and beliefs is a seminal characteristic of any tyrannical movement or ideology. Indeed, it is characteristic of players from the Right as well as the Left, who seek to impose their views on others. This usually extends to intimidation and shutting down of opposing speech, ("hate speech" it is called). Peter Boghossian, assistant professor of philosophy at Portland State University, experienced this when he was forced to resign as a critic of wokeness on campus. He describes the growing intolerance on his campus as the result of the far-left "ideology mill," that is intolerant of opposing views. In response to a question, "What is the ideology that fuels this kind of intolerance,?" he answers,

> "It depends on how academic you want to be. If you want to be more academic, in their book, *Cynical Theories*, Helen Pluckrose and James Lindsay call it 'critical social justice'. It has been more broadly termed 'wokeism'. Usually, it's a suite of orthodoxies relating to things like race, gender and sexual orientation. It is based on identity markers... I started asking questions. Ideologues don't like questions. I didn't receive answers, or when I did they were flippant or dismissive. People looked at me as if I had some kind of moral problem, as opposed to just not having the right information. It was very bizarre. They thought that I had to be a bad person, because I was asking questions. There is always the same pattern. What happened to me is being repeated for everybody. Everything seems to be fine. Then you start asking questions and people look at you as an outsider or as the other. Maybe you speak publicly about it and then the accusations and the investigations come. There's just something disconcerting about the threat of being hauled in because you don't have the 'right' answers to questions. It's like Tolkien's Lidless Eye – it's always watching you, it's always there. It puts pressure on you to conform to the moral orthodoxy."[82]

**Destruction of Free Speech,**[83] through demonization and destruction of its enemies, rather than rational discourse and collaboration. We see this in the current cancel-culture, where individuals are "cancelled" as a way of

---

[82] "Universities are turning into ideology mills," *Spiked,* 17 September, 2021
[83] Jonathan Turley, "The Death of Free Speech," *The Washington Post,* October 14, 2012

69

discrediting (and even destroying) them, or to get them fired from their jobs, if they disagree with the conventional politically correct, "woke" conversation. Generally speaking, the slang term "woke" refers to a person who is alert to the presence of privilege in their own lives and, by extension, to challenges faced by people who lack that privilege. The hallmark mantra of wokeness is the use of the triad of terms "diversity, equity, and inclusion," which by themselves express admirable sentiments and values, but too often are enforced by intimidation and coercion. Thus, words may become more important than actual state of mind, belief, or opinion. One has only to speak the right words to be judged acceptable. This has become a weird preoccupation of leftist ideology, with woke language used to virtue-signal compassion for the unprivileged but taken to ridiculous lengths to enforce language such as describing women as "persons who can become pregnant, or might seek an abortion"[84] or objection to the use of "sexist" language, such as "master bedroom," "wife," or "husband." Even one's preferred pronouns of identity must be asexual. Surely the intolerance of those who parse words towards those who fail the wokeness test is a testament of the hypocrisy and cruelty of this ideology.

Interestingly, the cancel culture has gone from association with the political Right in the 20th century (McCarthyism—Hollywood blacklist, etc.) to being associated with the Left in the 21st century. This goes to show that it is *false ideology*, not necessarily only an entity or party, that is the threat to our liberties.

**Dishonesty and Secrecy:** Tyranny thrives in the darkness of subterfuge and secrecy. Because it cannot survive rigorous intellectual scrutiny and transparent, open discussion, it relies on sleight-of-hand, distortion of the truth, and lies. Deception, illusion, misrepresentation, duplicity, trickery, and the sham are its trademarks.

Because tyranny manipulates and forces, it inevitably breeds reciprocal **resentment, envy, and hatred.**

---

[84] Nicole Ault, "The ACLU Decides 'Woman' Is a Bad Word," *Wall Street Journal*, October 3, 2021

Look carefully at the ideologies that you espouse. What are the underlying values that they advocate? Not the superficial ones and even the apparent ones. But the deep, foundational values and principles that operate predominately. Indeed, every sound, correct, right, and time-tested value and principle characteristic of freedom and liberty is antithetical to the totalitarian.

The traditional American values that have made the United States of American the greatest country on earth are under withering and unrelenting attack from those which seek to discredit these values, tear down American democracy, and replace it with a coercive, tyrannical socialism. There is no doubt about it: this group hates America and seeks to destroy it.

To do this, they are attacking the basic tenets, values, and principles that have made America great. They do this by insidiously substituting alternative values and principles that deceptively simulate but distort and pervert fundamental values of liberty. They capture our imagination by promising the utopian ideal of good for everyone, but cleverly disguise the coercive, devastating and vicious means to that end.

## Chapter 7: Foundations of American Democracy

American democracy was built upon five fundamental values/principles, three of which are on the face of every coin:

**Liberty**, that transcendent notion that empowers and magnifies the agency of man.

**In God we Trust**, which enshrines the crucial knowledge of the divine identity and destiny of man.

**E pluribus unum** (from many, one), the uniquely American tradition of bringing disparate peoples together in  a common culture of freedom and liberty.

**Truth**, the fundamental rock of meaning which facilitates unity of purpose.

**Virtue,** which is always triumphant--the lesson of the ages.

These tenets are the fundamental values and principles of the Western Judeo-Christian tradition. They are instinctively self-evident to mankind in its natural state. Most people respect liberty, freedom, truth, and virtue as an ultimate good. Humanity desperately wants to believe in God. This is evident that in every culture, there is a tradition of belief in a superior Power to which humans are accountable.

## Faith in God

The belief that there is a God, and that He is our Father, and that we are His children, is the fundamental conviction that undergirds all the hopes, dreams, aspirations, and actions of mankind. To know that He is real and the nature of our relationship to Him is what defines who we are, and what we may become, indeed, our very destiny. Without God, life is meaningless.

To know that God created humans to be free agents, but accountable to God for their actions is the essence of reality, and to understanding the world. God's revelation to man is the authoritative answer to moral, social, and political controversies that the wisdom of man will never be able to answer. This is another reason why the United States of America has become a great nation. Whenever individuals and nations recognize God as the Creator, as the Lawgiver, and choose to obey His commandments, they prosper. (See Chapter 8, A Brief Review of the Rise and Fall of Nations.) Solzhenitsyn again delivers this crucial insight:

> Over a half century ago, while I was still a child, I recall hearing a number of old people offer the following explanation for the great disasters that had befallen Russia: "Men have forgotten God; that's why all this has happened." Since then, I have spent well-nigh 50 years working on the history of our revolution; in the process I have read hundreds of books, collected hundreds of personal testimonies, and have already

contributed eight volumes of my own toward the effort of clearing away the rubble left by that upheaval. But if I were asked today to formulate as concisely as possible the main cause of the ruinous revolution that swallowed up some 60 millions of our people, I could not put it more accurately than to repeat: 'Men have forgotten God'; that's why all of this has happened.

## Liberty

"Give me liberty, or give me death!" The immortal words of Patrick Henry ring through the centuries as the soul-expression of mankind. Men were created to be free--to act and not to be acted upon. Liberty is the essential, crucial ingredient that empowers us to act with moral agency. It is the necessary element that enables a man or woman to rise to his/her full, creative, and unique potential and stature. The great strides of accomplishment in world history have always been made in the context of liberty of the individual exerting free agency to act anew and reveal a bright, shining jewel of truth that inspires all of mankind.

Men must be free to act; otherwise, as they are acted upon by an external force, their actions are a mere reflection of the will of another power. This is the central question of human civilization: in creating our utopia, will it be by the stultifying and suppressing force of coercion, or will it stimulate the highest aspirations and creative talents and energies of a free people? *This is what has made America the greatest nation on earth, leading the world in innovation, creation, and fostering the highest ideals of the human soul!*

Liberty and the expression of agency necessarily implies responsibility and accountability for one's actions. The freedom to act does not shelter us from the consequences of our actions. Thus, in a free society, there must be accountability and consequences for wrongful and destructive actions. The crucial difference from tyranny is that men are free to act in the first place, rather than to be forced or coerced. Tyrannical systems strangle that freedom, and thus shortcut responsibility and accountability for wrongful actions. Thus, the critical divergence of tyranny and liberty: the freedom to act rather than to be acted upon.

But we are losing our conception of liberty, and that puts us at great risk. Will we be willing to fight for our liberty?

(Liberty's ) old function was to render possible the emergence of values. Liberty pointed the way to virtue and heroism. That is what you have forgotten. Time has eroded your conception of liberty. You have retained the word and manufactured a new conception: the petty liberty that is only a caricature of the great, a liberty devoid of obligation and responsibility which leads, at best, to the enjoyment of material possessions. Nobody is prepared to die for that... If the object of freedom is narrowed to a conception of happiness that will only make humanity a hollow shell, people will sacrifice that freedom on some horrible altar or other. If it is directed to something greater, they just might. Too often it is only through suffering and the loss of freedom that one discovers the need for it and even what it's for.[85]

## E Pluribus Unum (From Many, One)

America is a nation of immigrants from many geographical points around the globe bringing diverse languages, ethnicities, and cultures together into a gigantic "melting pot," a phenomenon almost unheard of in the history of the world and certainly never on this scale. Their individualism and self-reliance, building their lives in a new world with the blessings of liberty, made America the great nation that it is.

As they came by the millions, they melded together the creation of the "American." This being came to represent typical American values of liberty, a Judeo-Christian tradition of belief in God, and unity out of diversity. By becoming an "American" each contributed to a new world culture, that of "Americanism."

America's melting pot is history's sole exception of E pluribus Unum inclusivity: a successful multiracial society bound by a common culture, language, and values.[86]

---

[85] Alexandr Solzhenitsyn, "Solzhenitsyn in Zurich," interview by Georges Suffert, *Encounter 46* (April 1976):14. (quoted in *Solzhenitsyn and American Culture,* edited by David P. Deavel and Jessica Hooten Wilson; University of Notre Dame Press, 2020, p45)

[86] Victor Davis Hansen, "Diversity: History's Pathway to Chaos," RealClearPolitics, 26 August 2016

Unfortunately, the mantra of "diversity is our strength" is today devolving into a pernicious and dangerous philosophy that divides rather than unites us.

> Today it is the Left that seeks to supplant E pluribus Unum with multiculturalism, which is preoccupied with race, ethnicity, and national origins and opposes the notion of one American identity.
>
> Hence the Left's preoccupation with "diversity," by which it means ethnic and racial diversity. "Diversity is our strength" is a Left-wing credo. It sounds true and admirable, but it is really an attempt to undo E Pluribus Unum by celebrating Pluribus, not Unum. Much of America's strength does indeed lie in its diverse origins, but America's strength is diminished by diverse primary identities. It is not diversity, but the ability to unify the diverse, that is America's strength and greatness.[87]

As diverse primary identities are highlighted in the new mantra of multiculturalism and identity politics, we become polarized into separate groups with diverging interests. This is evident in the new Leftist push for "Equity," which demands equality of outcome and special treatment of minority groups at the expense of the rest. The Left's "Identity Politics" creates victims and fosters divisions in a corrupt contrivance to gain power. In such competition among groups, we lose the "ability to unify the diverse".

The American experiment in democracy inspired the world to new heights of freedom and liberty. It ushered in an era of representative government unmatched in world history. But this tradition has become diluted and in many cases corrupted by the betrayal of the true values and principals upon which it was built. We see the concept of truth distorted and perverted into a narcissistic notion unhinged to reality. We see the ideal of real virtue as an anachronistic, self-serving righteousness, replaced by the phony virtue-signaling of the elites. As we look about us today we witness the tell-tale signs of a decaying culture that is losing its way and on the descending road to destruction.

---

[87] Prager, pp 375-376

# Chapter 8:  A Brief Review of the Rise and Fall of Nations

An ethical idea has always preceded the birth of a nation...And when with
the passage of time a nation's spiritual ideal is sapped, that nation falls,
together with all its civil statutes and ideals.[88] —Dostoevsky

There is a recurring pattern to the rise and fall of Nations--a predictable course: the rise of a great nation out of ethical and sound values and principles. Then, as prosperity, wealth and power accumulate, a generalized corruption infects the culture and, right at the peak of her greatness and glory, she self-destructs in catastrophic suicide. Such is the history of great nations, both of antiquity, and in recent times.

By studying these historical rise and fall patterns, we can perhaps catch a glimpse of what might be in store for us. A classic, enduring book on the rise and fall of the ancient republics, written by the Englishman Edward Wortley Montagu reminds us of what history can teach us:

> Our legislators can draw solid guidance only from studying the different constitutions of all the ancient republics and from sustained scrutiny of the circular path they followed from their birth to their fall. Hopefully, we will benefit and avoid the pitfalls that have left preceding nations in the dustheap of history. They will see that the most famous legislators of antiquity all preferred mixed governments, or governments made up of different powers which are in balance, and which keep each other within the bounds fixed by the constitution.

---

[88] Fyodor Dostoevsky, in his *Diary of a Writer;* quoted by Solzhenitsyn, "Repentance and Self-Limitation in the Life of Nations," *The Solzhenitsyn Reader, New and Essential Writings 1947-2005;* Edited by Edward E. Ericson, Jr., and Daniel J. Mahoney, ISI Books, 2006

They will see that liberty has never existed in states where there was only one sole power, because a single power is always absolute: they will be obliged to agree that exclusively popular governments have always been the least durable, the most liable to factiousness, the nearest to anarchy; that they can survive only among a people whose manners are still pure, and among whom the public virtues are still in their prime: but that a corrupted people is still enslaved under the freest of constitutions; because such people know of no other use for their liberty but to sell it.

All the republics of antiquity have in their turn demonstrated this sorrowful truth.[89]

From ancient Assyria through the recorded history of Egypt, Persia, Greece, Carthage, Rome, Islam, premodern Europe, Czarist Russia, Nazi Germany, Soviet Russia, Maoist China, the British Empire, and now, the United States of America, the pattern is the same. This pattern of the rise-and-fall of nations corresponds to the values and principles which their populations embraced. Chief among them is a belief in the accountability of man to a higher power (the religious sentiment and directive), and that pre-eminent lesson of the ages: virtue.

The story is well-documented by historians:

- Each of these nations (we will use Rome as the archetypical example) embodied a tradition of a belief in a Higher Power who dispensed moral directives, accountability of men to that power, and of hard work, conservative living, and connection to nature.

    The Romans founded their system of policy, at the very origin of their state, upon that best and wisest principle, 'The fear of the Gods, a firm belief of a divine superintending Providence, and a future state of rewards and punishments:' Their children were trained up in this belief from tender infancy, which took root and grew up with them by the influence of an excellent education, where they had the benefit of example as well as precept. Hence, we read of no heathen nation in the world, where both the publick and private duties of religion were so

---

[89] Montagu, Edward Wortley, *Reflections on the Rise and Fall of the Ancient Republics,* Liberty Fund, Inc. 2015, pp 271-272

strictly adhered to, and so scrupulously observed as amongst the Romans."

We find the same simplicity in their houses, diet and apparel; the same contempt for wealth, and quite to the last period of their liberty, the same warlike genius. Publick spirit and the love of their country was carried...to the highest pitch of enthusiasm...[90]

Even Cicero, the greatest orator of Caesar's day in Rome, and perhaps the most educated man of his day, at a time when Rome's pagan religion was waning, believed in this Higher Power.

(He believed in) the Being of a God; a Providence; the immortality of the soul; a future state of rewards and punishments; and the eternal difference of good and ill; ...He maintained that there was one God, or Supreme Being; ...who created the world by his power and sustained it by his providence. This he inferred from the consent of all nations; the order and beauty of the heavenly bodies; the evident marks of counsil (sic), wisdom, and a fitness to certain ends, observable in the whole, and in every part of the visible world; ...He believed also a divine Providence constantly presiding over the whole system, and extending its care to all the principal members of it, with a peculiar attention to the conduct and actions of men; He held likewise the immortality of the soul, and its separate existence after the death in a state of happiness or misery.[91]

- The fundamental social unit of each of these nations was the family: the union of a man and a woman nurturing, protecting, and teaching their children. A conspicuous exception to this were the Spartans who manifested other sound conservative values. But the lack of family cohesion contributed to the eventual corruption of their society that ended in the annihilation of their culture.
- Nations were built by the coalescing of family groups into communities that worked together in the interest of the whole. A sense of community and common interests bonded them together.

[90] Montagu. pp 192, 193
[91] Conyers Middleton, D. D., *The History of the Life of Marcus Tullius Cicero, Vol III, 5th Ed.*, London, printed for W. Innys and J. Richardson, in *Paternofter-Row;* R. Manby in the *Old-Bailey,* near *Ludgate-Hill;* and H.S. Cox in *Pater-noster Row;* MDCCLV, p 340-341

- The early Republics were representative governments that enshrined the principles of individualism, liberty and freedom.
- The populations of these nations became prosperous and wealthy through application of the virtues of hard work, self-reliance, and caring for one's neighbor.
- As wealth and luxury were introduced into societies, the manners of the population coarsened, and the love of money predominated, leading to avarice, pride, class distinctions and division.

> Before,...the Romans were poor, but they were contented and happy, because they knew no imaginary wants; and whilst their manners were virtuous, poverty itself was honourable, and added a new lustre to every other virtue. But when once they had contracted a relish for the luxury of Asia, they quickly found that the wealth of Asia was necessary to support it; and this discovery as quickly produced a total change in their manners. Before that time the love of glory, and a contempt of wealth, was the ruling passion of the Romans. Since that time, money was the only object of their applause and desire. Before, ambition impelled them to war, from a thirst of dominion; now avarice, for the sake of plunder to support the expense of luxury. Before, they seemed a race of Heroes; they were now a gang of insatiable robbers. Formerly, when they had reduced a people to obedience, they received them as their allies; they now made the conquered Nations their slaves. They fleeced the Provinces, and oppressed their friends.[92]

> Religion, justice, modesty, decency, all regard for divine or human laws, were swept away at once by the irresistible torrent of corruption. The nobility strained the privileges annexed to their dignity, and the people their liberty, alike into the most unbounded licentiousness. Everyone made the dictates of his own lawless will his only rule of action. Publick virtue, and the love of their country, which had raised the Romans to the empire of the universe, were extinct. Money which alone could enable them to gratify their darling luxury, was substituted in their place. Power, dominion, honours, and universal respect, were annexed to the possession of money. Contempt, and whatever was most reproachful, was the bitter portion of poverty; and to be poor, grew to

---

[92] Montagu, pp 170-171

be the greatest of all crimes in the estimation of the Romans. Thus, wealth and poverty contributed alike to the ruin of the Republick.[93]

- Secularization of the culture and loss of the religious sentiment.

    All attentive students of history must have noticed that, among all the nations which have successively disappeared from the surface of the globe, vice and corruption had their birth and pursued their fatal course in proportion to the scorn expressed for religious beliefs. When the Romans began to despise their gods and their oracles, they also lost a great deal of their military merit and were not long in losing respect for good faith in treaties and human conventions.[94]

    As long as the manners of the Romans were regulated by this first great principle of religion, they were free and invincible. But the Atheistical doctrine of Epicurus, which insinuated itself at Rome, under the respectable name of Philosophy, after their acquaintance with the Greeks, undermined and destroyed this ruling principle...luxury, by corrupting manners, had weakened this principle, and prepared the Romans for the reception of Atheism, which is the never-failing attendant of luxury. But as long as this principle remained, it controuled (sic) manners, and checked the progress of luxury, in proportion to its influence. But when the introduction of Atheism had destroyed this principle, the great bar to corruption was removed, and the passions at once let loose to run their full career without check, or countroul (sic). The introduction therefore of the Atheistical tenets attributed to Epicurus, was the real cause of that rapid depravity of the Roman manners.[95]

- Corruption of government followed the corruption of the populace, leading to conflict, polarization, envy, hatred, and strife.

    As an universal selfishness is the genuine effect of universal luxury, so the natural effect of selfishness is to break through every tye, both divine and human, and to stick at no kind of excesses in the pursuit of wealth, its favourite object. Thus the effects of selfishness will naturally appear in irreligion, breach of faith, perjury, a contempt of all the social

---

[93] Ibid. p 174
[94] Ibid. p 273
[95] Ibid. pp 196,197

duties, extortion, frauds in our dealings, pride, cruelty, universal venality and corruption.[96]

- Proliferation of laws to mitigate the evils and selfishness of a decaying culture.

  Many sumptuary laws were made to restrain the various excesses of luxury; but these efforts were too feeble to check the overbearing violence of the torrent.[97]

  The wisest and most complete legal code cannot reach all reprehensible actions, having no purchase on either feelings or the will. Fear of the laws may prevent a man from committing a crime in public, but it will never be enough to inspire in him the love of virtue.[98]

- Economic collapse followed years of profligate and unsustainable spending. The economic base of revenue-producing citizens from their own labour was gradually and insensibly reduced due to expansion of the welfare state until the culture could no longer sustain the expense of free stuff and services.

- Loss of faith among the populace in the societal institutions of government, and then a general disregard for the rule of law. We see this today as we are losing confidence in the institutions of our government as they fail in their appointed duties: the justice department, the FBI, the presidency, the Congress, and lately, even the scientific community, together with a generalized disillusionment in organized religion, that in many cases has become likewise corrupted.

- Tribal division of the populace. As divided political discourse takes hold, society becomes more and more polarized, retreating to the irrational defense of particular groups. This is characterized by a

---

[96] Ibid. p 177
[97] Ibid. p 181
[98] Montagu. p 274

prominent contemporary author, Ayaan Hirsi Ali, who has personal experience in her native Somalia, where tribalism has dominated the culture.

(A) blind hatred of a (a different) particular group... and the use of deeply personal attacks on individual(s)...to justify that hatred... The deeply divided society we now live in increasingly reminds me of clan or tribal behavior in Africa...suspicious of anyone from a different clan...to be guarded against anyone that was the 'other'...In tribal communities, neutral institutions of civil society that Westerners take for granted—such as the police, impartial courts, and the rule of law—simply do not, and cannot, exist. In such societies, everything is tribalized, and the task of building civic institutions is laden with difficulties."[99]

- Rise of tyrants and strong men to restore order and unify the people. This is what happened in Rome at the time of Caesar. Caesar recommended himself as a special case with dictatorial powers to rescue Rome from chaos and civil war. He suspended the laws of the Republic ostensibly to save it, but instead consigned it to totalitarian slavery.

"For this is the common effect of breaking through the barrier of the laws, by which many states have been ruined; when, from a confidence in the abilities and integrity of some eminent Citizen, they invest him, on pressing occasions, with extraordinary powers, for the common benefit and defence of the society: for though power so entrusted may in particular cases be of singular service, and sometimes even necessary; yet the example is always dangerous, furnishing a perpetual pretense to the ambitious and ill-designing, to grasp at every prerogative which had been granted at any time to the virtuous, till the same power, which would save a country in good hands, oppresses it at last in bad.[100]

Then, in a warning to our own times when a powerful savior rises to the rescue, and we bestow extraordinary power that in time turns to tyranny:

---

[99] Ayaan Hirsi Ali, "Tribalism has Come to the West," https://unherd.com/2021/05/tribalism-has-come-to-the-west/

[100] Conyers Middleton, *The History of the Life of M. Tullius Cicero, Vol I*, p 135-136

> (Then), a military government will be established upon the ruins of the civil, and all commands and employments will be disposed of at the arbitrary will of lawless power. The people will be fleeced to pay for their own fetters, and doomed, like the cattle, to unremitting toil and drudgery for the support of their tyrannical masters...the people will be compelled to give a sanction to Tyranny by their own suffrages, and to elect oppressors instead of protectors.[101]

- The people suffer under a tyrannical government until the tyranny collapses of its own corruption into chaos and anarchy (the fall of the Roman Empire), is subdued by another military power (the Greek Empire), or the populace rises in revolution and tears down the tyrannical government (the French revolution, Czarist Russia, to name only two).

Thus, we see a recurring pattern in the rise and fall of nations. In our own time, there seems to be a general awareness that our culture is on the wane and that we may have reached the nadir of our history. This surely reflects a lack of confidence in the values and principles that we have adopted, or a fearful awareness of those that we have betrayed and rejected. This conflicted diffidence and intuitive doubting not only threatens our ability to appreciate our freedoms, but also to defend them vigorously and passionately. Will we fight for our freedom? I believe that in a renewed commitment to discern what is true and what is false at the source of our ideologies we may find the confidence, certainty of conviction, and strength and means to preserve our liberty.

---

[101] Montagu, p 181

# Chapter 9:  The Faces of Modern Tyranny

O ur democracy seems to be morphing into an elitist, socialistic, oligarchic and authoritarian form of rule that seeks to impose a top-down, elitist agenda down our throats through a corruption of the normal representative process. The power base for this project includes the increasingly secular and left-leaning government bureaucracy, the postmodern, neomarxist leftist ideologues, the progressive Left, the leftist academia of the universities, the dogmatic Right establishment that is out to protect its privileges and power, and also the mega-corporations and the corporate media. Kaplan explains, "(T)he increasingly dense ganglia of international corporations and markets...are becoming the unseen arbiters of power... Corporations are like the feudal domains that evolved into nation-states; they are nothing less than the vanguard of a new Darwinian organization of politics."[102] This corporate/government alignment exerts tremendous influence through the inordinate power that big corporations wield. We used to view corporate America as the friend of free-market capitalism. But, driven by leftist 'woke' ideology, greed, and the power of market dominance (to be fair, greed is no exclusive property of the Left—the Right are just as prone) they have perverted the capitalistic incentive into a power-and-profit-driven despotism of authoritarian ideology.

Large portions of the public seem to be swallowing this perilous and treacherous path as they accede to the new 'woke" culture of intimidation, coercion and the abandonment of traditional American values and sound principles in favor of expediency and the authoritarian impulse to power. Thus, the face of modern tyranny is taking shape as individuals are tolerating,

---

[102] Robert D. Kaplan, *The Coming Anarchy;* Random House, 2000; p 80, 81

accepting, and submitting to the growing elitist and tyrannical philosophy of the Left and the Right that is shaping our culture every day. Add to this individuals of any stripe that seek to gain power by unsavory methods, and the violent extremists of both the Right and the Left. This includes you and me to the extent that we succumb to it and to the tyranny of our own personal, uninformed and biased opinions that are not anchored in truth.

Tyrannical ideology distorts or ignores facts, corrupts or abandons correct values and principles, and disparages faith in God in its ravenous and greedy thirst for power. Values of compassion and fairness ("for the people") are deceitfully trumpeted while disparaging liberty and agency as secondary to an expediency that favors a worthy end ("the end justifies the means"). This is what is happening in America today—an insidious, vicious attempt to distort, repress, and corrupt traditional American values, and if unchecked will destroy the American system as we know it.

The forces of tyranny and totalitarianism can be recognized by their negation of every one of the founding principles of our nation. These values and principles are anathema to the radical left and to the radical right. A careful examination of the values/principles of these groups reveals elemental incompatibility with these traditional American values. Indeed, while speaking in the language of virtue, equality, fairness, and good, the Leftist philosophy of atheism, relativism, equity, social justice and that of the violent extremists of the Right and the Left are absolutely contradictory and irreconcilable to liberty and freedom. *Thus, we are engaged in an existential culture war of differing values and principles. The only solution to our dilemma is a fundamental break from false ideology in favor of elemental truth.*

Following are some of the tyrannical trends that are rapidly shaping our culture, leading us to a modern and uniquely American tyranny:

**The secularization of American culture.**  When we reject God as our protector and lawgiver, and cease to look to Him for our guide and our strength, we lose the sure connection to truth and reality and the power of His protecting and sustaining hand. The new atheistic postmodern philosophy has infiltrated and transformed the academic intelligentsia and is now corrupting our entire educational system, tutoring our children in the propaganda of the radical Left.

**The collapse of moral and ethical values** that leaves us adrift in our quest for what is right and what is wrong. Three salient issues demonstrate this: (1) The thriving abortion industry which rejects the sacredness of Life, (2) The widespread acceptance of gay marriage as an alternative to the traditional God-established family unit of a father and mother raising and teaching their children, and (3) the legalization of and pervasive use of mind-altering, hallucinogenic drugs that corrupt and destroy the individual's ability to discern reality, and to exercise his agency to act. Add to this the pervasive exploitation of sex, the overflowing scourge of pornography, the preoccupation with the pathetic and banal, superficial and trivial, and the clichéd, debauched trivialization of blood and murder in the entertainment industry; the corruption of our morals as we reject the fundamental virtues and moral laws that are essential to healthy family life.

Jordan Peterson warns that "the collapse of values is a far greater danger than climate change." Then we are left prey to the impulse of power and coercion in a mad scramble for dominance. This is the story of the suicide of Greece from the Peloponnesian wars, a direct result of the coarseness of manners and rejection of a moral code. We see this now in the lack of respect and care for our neighbor, and the ugly demonization of those who disagree with us as we descend into the new tribalism of conflict and polarization. Solzhenitsyn decries the amoralization of our politics by those who say, "'We cannot apply moral criteria to politics.' Thus we mix good and evil, right and wrong, and make space for the absolute triumph of absolute evil in the world. Only moral criteria can help the West against communism's well-planned world strategy. There are no other criteria."[103]

**The substitution of ideology for truth.** The lazy-man's barter for phony certitude.

---

[103] Quoted by Solzhenitsyn, "Harvard Address, June 8, 1978; *The Solzhenitsyn Reader, p 570*

**The substitution of truth with irrational "will to believe."** It's common to claim one's "own truth" based on "feeling, instinct, or leaps of faith."[104] This is usually uninformed opinion that is deemed pre-eminent. It has no tether to what is actually real. It translates into an irrational "will to believe" that relies on the idea "that one's feelings and passions are better guides than reason,"[105] and the warped concept that experience *is* truth rather than the reality that experience *informs* truth. This insidious idea has permeated American thinking and culture.

**The collapse of the family unit** portends a society without filial love and intimacy, the wellsprings of individual identity and confident and secure personality, and the durable strength of the nation as a whole. Recent research reveals the dire straits that the institution of the family suffers in our day:

> For millennia the family has stood as the central institution of society—often changing, but always essential. But across the world, from China to North America, and particularly in Europe, family ties are weakening...
>
> Margaret Mead once said, "no matter how many communes anyone invents, the family always creeps back." But today's trajectory is not promising. Even before the Covid-19 pandemic, family formation and birth rates were declining throughout much of the world...Our societies have become increasingly lonely, with single men hit hardest and children, often without two parents or any siblings, and chained to social media, increasingly isolated around the world. In the U.S. sine 1960, the percentage of people in the United States living alone has grown from about 12 percent to 28 percent. Even intimacy is on its way out, particularly among the young; the once swinging age groups now are suffering a "sex recession." The percentage of American women who are mothers is at its lowest point in over three decades. Intact families are rarer, and single living more common. In the United States, the rate of single parenthood has grown from 10 percent to over 40 percent today...The social collapse is going global.
>
> A woke utopia, where children and families are rare, upward mobility constrained, and society built around a collective welfare system, would create a society that rewards hedonism and personal self-absorption. There is nothing as binding in a society as the ties created by children, who give us reason to fight against an encroaching dystopia.[106]

---

[104] Hicks, *Explaining Postmodernism,* p 57
[105] Ibid, p 181
[106] Joel Kotkin, "The Fading Family," *The American Mind,* 09.07.2021

**The increasingly authoritarian impulse** to intimidate and coerce people to do what their betters want them to do. Rather than teaching correct values and sound principles and changing peoples' hearts, the contemporary urge is to *change the system* to manipulate and compel people to do the right thing.

**The suppression of free speech** characterized by the absurd and destructive "cancel culture" and the corruption and censorship of the corporate media, as well as escalating governmental efforts to control speech, such as the Department of Justice's recent memo threatening free speech at school board meetings.[107] Many see this as a sinister impulse to limit a fundamental freedom in an effort to gain power (which it really is), but the Left looks at this from a view that free speech is a physical construct that needs to be limited in order to achieve safety and fairness. (Again, the use of the word "fairness"). This derives from their core beliefs that "reason (speech) is socially constructed (and) not a tool of knowing reality"; that speech is a "form of social conditioning that makes us who we are"—pawns without volition and products of our social environments. "Postmodernism...presupposes a social subjectivist epistemology, a social-determinist view of human nature, and an altruistic, egalitarian ethic. Speech codes are a logical application of those beliefs."[108]

The **trend towards socialism** which is a form of authoritarian and necessarily atheistic, rule. Dostoevsky reminds us that "...socialism of any type and shade leads to a total destruction of the human spirit and to a leveling of mankind into death."[109]

**Identity politics** that sows envy and division, judging persons not by "the content of their character" but by ethnic, sexual, and racial grouping—*the new racism*. This is leading to the **division and polarization** of our society that threatens our ability to live together in peace, reminiscent of the days before the Civil War.

---

[107] Merrick Garland, Attorney General of the United States, "Memorandum" for Law Enforcement, October 4, 2021; see also: Andrew McCarthy, "The Biden Justice Department's lawless threat against American parents," *National Review,* October 5, 2021

[108] Hicks, "Free Speech & Postmodernism," *Explaining Postmodernism,* p 239

[109] Solzhenitsyn, "Harvard Address", June 8, 1978

**The addictive passion for the false and phony "virtual reality" of computer-chip technology**, especially among the young people, who are vulnerable to a false conception of reality as they engage in hours and hours of video-game entertainment.

**The passion and obsession with what money can buy—***the perversion of capitalism by greed.* The appetite for the modern technology that substitutes material prosperity for spiritual growth and distracts us from discerning the growing decadence around us. This involves public policy as well as private. Massive, unprecedented government spending and debt in the vain and futile hope of solving society's problems by throwing money at them.

**Loss of confidence in the integrity of voting**, as competing parties attempt to manipulate and game the system to their own advantage. This is an ominous development after the recent elections, and must be laid at the feet of both parties.

**The corruption of the justice system** by the proliferation of laws attempting to make bad men good, and the unequal application of the laws, favoring the elite and corporate class with means to buy influence. Indeed, the very flouting of the laws as corrupt officials systematically fail to execute the laws (i.e. "defund the police" and the "smash and grab" phenomenon that is rampant in U.S. cities).

I have often noticed the sterile, overly legalistic intellectualism of the new legal scholarship. This is not just detailed and precise speech, but a betrayal of the higher, intangible aspects of human lives. Solzhenitsyn saw this first-hand:

"I have spent all my life under a Communist regime and I will tell you that a society without any objective legal scale is a terrible one indeed. But a society with no other scale but the legal one is also less than worthy of man. A society based on the letter of the law and never reaching any higher fails to take advantage of the full range of human possibilities. The letter of the law is too cold and formal to have a beneficial influence on society. Whenever the tissue of life is woven of legalistic relationships, this creates an atmosphere of spiritual mediocrity that paralyzes man's noblest impulses."[110]

The **economic stagnation** and **shrinking** of the middle class, as the culture becomes increasingly divided into the very rich and the very poor. The economic health of the middle class is losing ground to increasing taxation and inflation. The American middle class has traditionally represented "empowered political citizenship,"[111] the key to social stability and upward mobility which has made the American economy and culture the envy of and example to the world of a vibrant and expanding prosperity never matched before. Now, the middle class face an "era of middle-class economic insecurity and uncertainty."[112] This endangers the stability and prosperity of the nation as a whole.

The **accumulation of data** of individuals exploited by government for behavior control. This is already a major project in China and is represented here by the unholy alliance of the corporate media with government bureaucracy.

The **dying concept of citizenship** manifested in the indifference, passivity, and disinterest we show towards engaging in the political process and protecting our liberties, as described by Victor Davis Hansen in his new book, *The Dying Citizen.*

Each of these trends is in full display as we observe the contemporary culture of our day. Could each of them  be turned around by a return to the source point of "What is true?" and "What is not true?"

## We are responsible for the path our country follows

These days, many feel powerless as individuals to affect the future of our country. Larger and more pervasive forces, seemingly beyond our control, are

---

[110] Solzhenitsyn, "Harvard Address"
[111] Victor Davis Hansen, *The Dying Citizen,* Basic Books, 2021, p 30
[112] Ibid. p 37

determining events. And yet, we must realize that these forces are merely the aggregation of individual attitudes, choices, and actions. Yes, *we*, as individuals, are the destiny of our country. We will be the face of modern tyranny, or of the rebirth of American freedom and liberty.

Alexandr Solzhenitsyn, who survived Stalinist Russia and the collapse of the Soviet Union, understood as well as anyone of his time how individuals indeed control and are responsible for, the evolution of their country. Speaking of Russia, but certainly pertinent to our own time and country, he asserts that each of us is accountable:

> Even when the majority of the population is quite powerless to obstruct its political leaders, it is fated to answer for their sins and their mistakes. Even in the most totalitarian states, whose subjects have no rights at all, we all bear responsibility—not only for the quality of our government, but also for the campaigns of our military leaders, for the deeds of our soldiers in the line of duty, for the shots fired by our frontier guards, for the songs of our young people...
>
> For half a century now we have acted on the conviction that the *guilty* ones were the tsarist establishment, the bourgeois patriots, social democrats, White Guards, priests, emigres, subversives, kulaks, henchmen of kulaks, engineers, 'wreckers,' oppositionists, enemies of the people, nationalists, Zionists, imperialists, militarists, even modernists—anyone and everyone except you and me!...
>
> This realm of darkness, of falsehood, of brute force, of justice denied and distrust of the good, this slimy swamp was formed by *us*, and no one else. We grew used to the idea that we must submit and lie in order to survive, and we brought up our children to do so. Each of us, if he honestly reviews the life he has led, without special pleading or concealment, will recall more than one occasion on which he pretended not to hear a cry for help, averted his indifferent eyes from an imploring gaze, burned letters and photographs which it was his duty to keep, forgot someone's name or dropped certain widows, turned his back on prisoners under escort, and—but of course—always voted, rose to his feet, and applauded obscenities (even though he felt obscene while was doing it)—how, otherwise, could we survive? How, moreover, could the great Archipelago have endured in our midst for fifty years unnoticed?
>
> We are all guilty, all besmirched...*We, all of us,* Russia herself, were the necessary accomplices.[113]

---

[113] Solzhenitsyn, "Repentance and Self-Limitation in the Life of Nations"; essay contributed to the 1974 collection, *From Under the Rubble.*

We must realize that each of us adds strength to forces of good or evil as we as *individuals* accept and participate in untruth, either unknowingly, unwittingly, ignorantly, or out of confusion, deception, or intentional ignorance, or even simple laziness. Or out of fear! We are part of it. Our own countenance and image then will become enshrined in the mosaic of the faces of modern tyranny. Will the *face of modern tyranny be the face we look at in the mirror every day?*

Our hope lies in the invincible and irrepressible goodness of the human spirit. Each of us has the power and choice to rise above the deceptions, manipulations and coercions of our day. As we claim the high road of faith in God, of virtue, of liberty, and freedom—of truth—we will save our country. And we will each be a hero for the generations to come.

# Chapter 10:  The Tyranny of Uninformed Personal Opinion

L et me state a simple fact: Unless our opinions and beliefs are based on truth, we are each vulnerable to the tyranny of ideology. We become the face of modern tyranny.

This is a hard verity to face.

We may be holding onto opinions and beliefs that are not based on reality. Is it possible that we have not taken the crucial action of subjecting our precious ideology to a honest and rigorous examination of whether or not it is based on truth? Have we subjected it carefully to reliable standards of truth?

Is it consistent with the facts? Have we taken the time  and effort to inform ourselves of the known facts of the matter?

Is it consistent with correct values and sound principles? What are the values and principles that we subscribe to? Have we sacrificed a primary, crucial value or principle to a secondary one, such as agency to equality?

Is it consistent with God-given revelation? Have we consulted the revelations of God to His prophets, His voice recorded in scripture, and most important of all, that supreme, tender, and sacred still, small voice within?

These are questions we need to honestly ask ourselves.

What is a man or woman willing to give up, dispelling his/her mind of the debris of bias, prejudice and dogmatism? What will he/she give up to free himself/herself of the tyranny of his/her own ideology? When will he/she humble himself/herself in a complete, free-willed surrender to what is true?

This is the mark of true character, as Emerson says of Socrates, "...a shrewdness which (will) not suffer itself to be duped...(and) the faculty which enables (one) to investigate his own character, to learn the natural tendency and bias of his own genius, and thus to perfectly control his mental energies."[114]

Let me state this clearly and unequivocally: *I have no ideology. I'm only interested in what is true, as best as I can discern it.* I have no interest in vain, biased and uninformed opinions and beliefs that have no anchor in the truth.

This is my declaration:

*"I will give up my pride, my vain ambition, my precious opinions that comfort me and make me feel good because they are easy to believe, or appeal to some selfish or personal quirk. I will give up my own wisdom in favor of the greater wisdom of God. I will give up my own compulsion to follow my own carnal nature in favor of what God has commanded. I will give up my own mortal conception of what my life should be in favor of what God wills it to be. I will give all that I have in favor of what is true."*

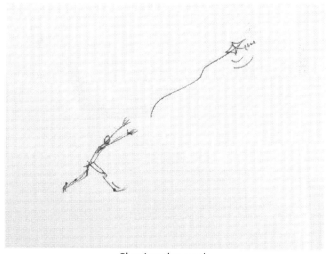

Chasing the truth

---

[114] Emerson, Ralph Waldo, *Two Unpublished Essays: The Character of Socrates, The Present State of Ethical Philosophy,* Lamson, Wolffe, & Co., 1895, p 12-13.

# Chapter 11:  Love, Repentance, and Forgiveness

"A believing love will relieve us of a vast load of care.
O my brothers, God exists."
--Ralph Waldo Emerson, Essay on Spiritual Laws[115]

As I read the news each day, I find it filled with contention, hatred and demonization of opponents. A cursory scan of the news: "___ slammed so-and-so", "___ rips ___", "___ calls out ___", "___takes a shot at ___", "...burn, slash, and loot.", "___stomps on ___", "___knocks ___", "Any idiot ...", ad nauseam. How could anyone feel motivated to change for the better from such blather? How will we ever achieve any measure of unity as we judge, trash, harass, and persecute one another? The contemporary "cancel culture" seeks to destroy persons who have simply made a mistake, no matter how long ago, no matter how much they have apologized, no matter how they have changed. A contrary view is a sure call for the "politics of personal destruction."

Much of the current contention is over America's sins of the past, but also those of the present. The legacy of slavery and exploitation of Native Americans continues to haunt the soul of America. The Left has used these mistakes to instill "White Guilt,"[116] and then exploit that guilt in divisive, polarizing claims of "systemic racism" at every turn and demands for punishment and

---

[115] Ralph Waldo Emerson, "Spiritual Laws"; *The Essays of Ralph Waldo Emerson,* The Illustrated Modern Library, 1994, by Random House, Inc.; p 82
[116] From Shelby Steele, *White Guilt, How Blacks and Whites Together Destroyed the Promise of the Civil Rights Era;* Harper Perennial, 2006, p 24

reparations in their relentless ambition to gain power. The civil rights movement of the sixties was a genuine effort by the nation at large to acknowledge the sins of slavery of the past and codify the laws to prevent such sins of "systemic racism" in the future. These effort were largely successful in removing systemic racism in our country (although individual instances of racism sadly continue to occur). The nation's acknowledgment of the civil rights movement can be viewed as an act of "repentance" for the sins of slavery. But this wasn't enough for the hucksters of the Left, who continue to cry "racism" at every turn to exploit the sins of the past to gain and perpetuate their political power. Mr. Steele, author of *White Guilt,* contends, "For black leaders in the age of white guilt the problem was how to seize all they could get from white guilt *without* having to show actual events of racism. Global racism was the answer. With it, the smallest racial incident proved the 'global truth' of systemic racism."[117]

This language of the Left crying "systemic racism," "white supremacy," "white privilege," and the language of victimization they use when referring to minority groups is nothing more than the politics of tribalism, of polarization to the extent that rational discourse has become impossible. Hatred and irrational fear of our enemy from the Left and the Right have replaced patience, understanding, and compromise. We have diverged so far that unity seems impossible.

What is the cure? The antidote? ANSWER: *To love our neighbor*! And to *reclaim the vision of our true identity—who we truly are, and of our destiny*! Fyodor Dostoevsky in *The Brothers Karamazov* quotes a peasant woman seeking to get back her faith:

> How? (to get back my faith)
> 'By the experience of active love. Strive to love your neighbour actively and tirelessly. In so far as you advance in love you will grow surer of the reality of God and of the immortality of your soul...This has been tried. This is certain.[118]

---

[117] Steele, p 36
[118] Fyodor Dostoevsky, *The Brothers Karamazov;* The Easton Press, 1979, p 40

I am loath to demonize my friends when they disagree with me. No friendship is worth the losing over a disagreement about political or moral philosophy. Yes, I abhor the philosophy of Leftism—as well as the betrayal of the Right when it fails to preserve conservative values, and I may dislike the actions of individuals that are contrary to my values. But I will seek to see the inherent goodness of every human being that is my brother or sister and treat him or her with respect as a son or daughter of God. "Can the spirit of generosity be extended any more widely? If people were able to feel some generosity in interpreting the remarks of others, even of those on an opposing side, then some lessening of the trench-digging might be possible,"[119] asserts Douglas Murray in his recent book, *The Madness of* Crowds. I will pray for the ability to love my enemies—to see the value they hold apart from our differences. I will pray for strength to forgive, as I seek to be forgiven. Yes, people can change—I have changed! I will seek truth over ideology and personal interest. This, I believe, is the only path towards reconciliation and mutual understanding that is necessary for us to achieve unity in a world full of contention.

"It is now only too obvious how dearly mankind has paid for the fact that we have all throughout the ages preferred to censure, denounce, and hate *others*, instead of censuring, denouncing, and hating ourselves. But obvious though it may be, we are even now, with the twentieth century on its way out, reluctant to recognize that the universal dividing line between good and evil runs not between countries, not between nations, not between parties not between classes, not even between good and bad men...It divides the heart of every man...

"...what way out remains to us? Not the embittered strife of parties or nations, not the struggle to win some delusive *victory*—for all the ferocious causes already in being—but simply *repentance* and the search for *our own* errors and sins. We must stop blaming everyone else—our neighbors and more distant peoples, our geographical, economic, or ideological rivals, always claiming that we alone are in the right.

"Repentance is the first bit of firm ground underfoot, the only one from which we can go forward not to fresh hatreds but to concord. Repentance is the only starting point for spiritual growth.

"For each and every individual."[120]

---

[119] Douglas Murray, *The Madness of Crowds*; Bloomsbury Continum, 2019; p 252
[120] Solzhenitsyn, "Repentance and Self-Limitation in the Life of Nations"

This goes back to the elemental truth of the universe: God exists, and we are His children, created in His image. As we accept that great truth, a path is opened, and a vision appears, of who we really are, and who we may become: the divine destiny of man. Then, we can move forward united in the cause of the betterment of mankind. With eyes to see and ears to hear, we will discern the truths and capture the power that will surely keep us free.

# Chapter 12: Truth Revisited

The greatest adventure that you can possibly have is the one that you find if you look for the truth.
    —Jordan Peterson

The fleeting glimpses that I have been able to have of truth can hardly convey an idea of the indescribable luster of truth, a million times more intense than that of the Sun we daily see with our eye. In fact, what I have caught is only the faintest glimmer of that mighty effulgence.[121]

Therefore, the pursuit of truth is... the path that leads to God. There is no place in it for cowardice, no place for defeat. It is the talisman by which death itself becomes the portal to life eternal.[122] —Mahatma Gandhi

And so, we have come full circle. The essence of our problem is that we are forgetting God. We all know this. Even the children—and especially the old people with life experience—know it best.

A living belief in God will give you and me the courage and the commitment to look for the truth of things in every situation. We must cast off our false, pathetic, and lame ideologies, and grow up as men and women of character, of integrity, with the fortitude and courage to accept and embrace the reality of things as they really are.

---

[121] Mahatma Gandhi, *"The Way to God", Selected Writings from Mahatma Gandhi,* Edited by M.S. Deshpande, North Atlantic Books, 2009, p 67
[122] Ibid. p 28

Our life consists not in the pursuit of material success but in the quest for worthy spiritual growth. Our entire earthly existence is but a transitional stage in the movement toward something higher, one rung of the ladder. Material laws alone do not explain our life or give it direction. The laws of physics and physiology will never reveal the indisputable manner in which the Creator constantly, day in and day out, participates in the life of each of us, unfailingly granting us the energy of existence; when this assistance leaves us, we die. And in the life of our entire planet the Divine Spirit surely moves with no less force: This we must grasp in our dark and terrible hour.

To the ill-considered hopes of the last two centuries, which have reduced us to insignificance and brought us to the brink of nuclear and non-nuclear death, we can propose only a determined quest for the warm hand of God, which we have so rashly and self-confidently spurned. Only in this way can our eyes be opened to the errors of this unfortunate twentieth century and our hands be directed to setting them right. There is nothing else to cling to in the landslide: The combined vision of all the thinkers of the Enlightenment amounts to nothing.

Our five continents are caught in a whirlwind. But it is during trials such as these that the highest gifts of the human spirit are manifested. If we perish and lose this world, the fault will be ours alone.[123] —Alexandr Solzhenitsyn

I end my narrative with an invitation to you, gentle reader, with gratitude for your patience, steadfastness and perseverance in staying with me thus far.

I invite you to carefully take another serious look at your innermost, most precious opinions and beliefs, your own particular *ideology*, and the ideologies with which you identify, in an ardent and zealous resolve and commitment to align them to the rock of truth in every situation. Will you join me today in this marvelous, exhilarating and transcending path to freedom and liberty?

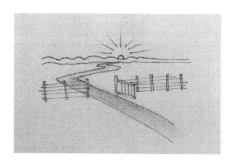

[123] Alexandr Solzhenitsyn, "Templeton Lecture, London, Guildhall, May 10, 1983

# BIBLIOGRAPHY

Bronowski, Jacob, *The Ascent of Man,* The Folio Society, London, MMXII.

Carter, Thomas M. *What Is Real? My Search for Truth in a World of Chaos and Confusion.* Amazon Kindle Direct Publishing, 2019.

de Montaigne, Michel, *Essays.* Translated by Donald M. Frame. The Franklin Library, 1979.

de Tocqueville, Alexis. *Democracy in America, Vol I ,* Alfred A. Knopf, 1945.

Deshpande, M. S., Editor. *The Way to God; Selected Writings from Mahatma Gandhi.* North Atlantic Books, Berkeley, California. 2009

Dostoevsky, Fyodor. *The Brothers Karamazov.* The Easton Press, 1979.

Emerson, Ralph Waldo. *The Essays of Ralph Waldo Emerson*. The Illustrated Modern Library. Random House, Inc. 1944

Emerson, Ralph Waldo, *Two Unpublished Essays: The Character of Socrates, The Present State of Ethical Philosophy,* Lamson, Wolffe, & Co., 1895

Ericson, Edward E. Jr, Mahoney, Daniel, Editors. *The Solzhenitsyn Reader.* ISI Books, 2006

Frankl, Viktor E. *Man's Search for Meaning.* Beacon Press, Boston. 2014.

Gairdner, William D. *The Great Divide: Why Liberals and Conservatives will Never, Ever Agree.* Encounter Books. 2015

Hanson, Victor David, *The Dying Citizen.* Basic Books, New York, 2021

Hicks, Stephen R. C. *Explaining Postmodernism.* Ockham's Razor Publishing. 2018.

Kaplan, Robert D. *The Coming Anarchy.* Random House, New York, 2000.

Kotkin Stephen. *Stalin, Waiting for Hitler, 1929-1941,* Penguin Press, 2017.

Levin, Mark R. *Liberty and Tyranny, A Conservative Manifesto,* Threshold Editions, 2009.

Middleton, Conyers, D.D. *The History of the Life of Marcus Tullius Cicero.* London: printed for W. Innys and J. Richardson, in *Paternofter-Row;* R. Manaby, in the *Old Bailey,* near *Ludgate-Hill*; and H.S. Cox, in *Paternofter-Row. MDCCLV.*

Mill, John Stuart. *On Liberty.* Easton Press, 1991

Montagu, Edward Wortley. *Reflections on the Rise and Fall of the Ancient*

*Republics.* THE CLASSICS OF LIBERTY LIBRARY, Gryphon Corporation. 2020.

Murray, Douglas, *The Madness of Crowds*, Bloomsbury Continuum, 2019

Plato. *The Republic.* Translated by A.D. Lindsay. The Franklin Library, 1975.

Prager, Dennis. *Still the Best Hope—Why the World Needs American Values to Triumph.* Broadside Books, 2012.

Sahakian, William S. and Sahakian, Mabel Lewis. *Ideas of the Great Philosophers.* Barnes & Noble, 1968.

Schweitzer, Albert. *Out of My Life and Thought, an Autobiography.* Copywrite 1933, 1949 by Henry Holt and Company, Inc; Easton Press, 1989

Shapiro, Ben. *The Authoritarian Moment.* Broadside Books, 2021.

Shirer, William L. *The Rise and Fall of the Third Reich, A History of Nazi Germany.* Simon and Shuster, 1960.

Simon, Roger L. *I Know Best: How Moral Narcissism is Destroying Our Republic If It Hasn't Already;* Encounter Books, 2016.

Solzhenitsyn, Aleksandr I. *THE GULAG ARCHIPELAGO, 1918-1956, An Experiment in Literary Investigation II-III*; Harper & Row, Publishers, 1975.

Steele, Shelby. *White Guilt, How Blacks and Whites Together Destroyed the Promise of the Civil Rights Era;* Harper Perennial, 2006.

*The Book of Mormon.* The Church of Jesus Christ of Latter-Day Saints, Salt Lake City, Utah.

*The Doctrine and Covenants of the Church of Jesus Christ of Latter-Day Saints.* The Church of Jesus Christ of Latter-Day Saints, Salt Lake City, Utah. 1989

*The Holy Bible,* King James version

Made in the USA
Monee, IL
16 January 2022

ccf9d605-34ec-4bcf-b659-4d013c0718b1R01